KU-226-166

PRECIOUS METAL CLAY

25 gorgeous designs for jewellery and gifts

XUELLA ARNOLD

Search Press

First published in the UK by
Search Press Ltd
Wellwood
North Farm Road
Tunbridge Wells
Kent TN2 3DR

NG 27-8-08.

Volume © 2008 by Breslich & Foss Ltd

ISBN 13: 978-1-84448-358-7

All rights reserved. No part of this book, text, photographs or illustrations,
may be reproduced, stored in a retrieval system, or transmitted, in any form
or by any means by print, photoprint, microfilm, microfiche, photocopier,
internet, or in any way known or as yet unknown, without the prior
permission in writing of the publisher.

Suppliers

If you have difficulty in obtaining any of the materials and equipment
mentioned in this book, please visit the Search Press website for details of
suppliers: www.searchpress.com

This book was conceived, designed and produced by
Breslich & Foss Ltd
2A Union Court
20-22 Union Road
London SW4 6JP

Printed in China

Text: Xuella Arnold
Photography: Martin Norris
Design: Janet James

PRECIOUS
METAL CLAY

LV 32762038

LIVERPOOL LIBRARIES

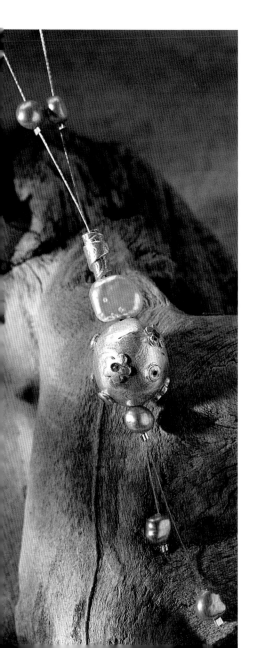

CONTENTS

INTRODUCTION

Because of its unique composition, precious metal clay is a revolutionary way of working in silver. It offers amazing opportunities for jewellery designers and makers to create highly individual, one-off pieces. Because it is such a new product, having first been introduced about a decade ago, I think there are still things to be discovered about it, which makes it a very exciting prospect.

Precious metal clay is ideal for creating detailed textures and for combining with other materials, such as ceramics, dichroic glass, stones, enamel, and gold foil. It cannot take the place of traditional silver techniques, but it can be used alongside them and combined with them, exploiting the unique properties of each material.

The projects and techniques in this book demonstrate some of the possibilities of precious metal clay, from the simplest ideas to quite complex designs. I hope that they will inspire you to create your own personalised pieces of jewellery.

Xuella Arnold

TOOLS AND MATERIALS

PRECIOUS METAL CLAY

Precious metal clay is a relatively new material. It is made up of microscopic pure silver particles in an organic binder with water. You can use it in exactly the same way as clay—roll it out, cut it, and mold it. When it has dried out and the water has evaporated, it can be fired, either in a kiln or with a torch. During firing the binder burns away, causing the piece to shrink slightly, and the silver particles fuse together (a process known as sintering), forming pure hallmark-quality fine silver, which has a higher silver content than sterling silver. Once it has been fired, it can be treated just as traditional silver.

There are three basic types of precious metal clay:

PMC STANDARD

This is the original precious metal clay. It shrinks by 30 percent during firing.
Pros: It is a very smooth clay and, because of the amount by which it shrinks, it can be used for finely detailed designs.
Cons: It is not as strong as newer forms of pmc and requires higher firing temperatures and longer firing times. It shrinks a lot (which can be an advantage).

PMC+

PMC+ can be fired at a lower temperature than standard pmc and can be combined with some stones. It shrinks by about 12 percent.
Pros: It shrinks less than standard pmc and is stronger; it can be soldered.
Cons: It is stiffer to use than standard pmc, because it contains less binder.

PMC3

This is the strongest and most versatile of the precious metal clays. It shrinks by 10–12 percent.
Pros: It is strong and can be fired at low temperatures, so it can be combined with other materials such as ceramic and glass. It is easy to solder on to.
Cons: It is the most expensive type of pmc.

PMC GOLD

The pure gold form of pmc can be combined with pmc3 silver.
Pros: It is good for using in small quantities for setting stones and has a great yellow gold colour.
Cons: pmc gold is very expensive. It requires a high firing temperature and a long firing time.

There are different forms of pmc. Clay is ready to use for rolling out and cutting out; all the types of clay listed come in this form. Slip (paste) is a more liquid form of the clay, which is used for coating and for joining pieces of clay together. Slip is available in both pmc+ and pmc3.

Syringe pmc is a paste form of clay, sold in ready-made syringes; it is used for piping designs and for joining pieces of clay together, and is available in pmc+ and pmc3. Sheet or paper pmc is a ready-made thin sheet of pmc+ that doesn't dry out. It can be used for origami or punched out with paper punches for decoration.

There is also a make of silver clay known as Artclay, which has slightly different properties from pmc. There is a special slow-drying clay and a type of paste. In this book I have used only precious metal clay, but many of the projects can be made with Artclay. Refer to the manufacturer's firing temperatures and recommendations.

TOOLS AND EQUIPMENT

These are some of the basic tools that you will need when working with pmc. There are other tools that you can acquire over time.

1 WORKBOARD

To roll out clay, you need a flat board that has a smooth, non-absorbent surface, such as glass or acrylic.

2 BADGER BALM

Available from some health-food stores, this is a balm that will stop the clay from sticking to your tools and hands. If you can't obtain it, you can substitute olive oil—but use it sparingly.

3 ROLLER

To roll out the clay to an even thickness, use a domestic rolling pin or any cylindrical object with a smooth, non-absorbent surface, such as acrylic or plastic. I have even used cut-off lengths of plastic plumbing pipe.

4 SPACERS

Place spacers to each side of the clay when you are rolling out to keep it an even thickness. Playing cards are perfect to use as spacers because you can alter the thickness very gradually.

5 CUTTING TOOLS

You can buy shaped cutters made especially for pmc or use cutters from cake-decorating and polymer-clay suppliers. For cutting out shapes of your own design, use a craft knife.

6 TEXTURE PLATES

Texture plates are used to impress a pattern or texture onto pmc. You can buy ready-made rubber or brass texture plates from pmc- and card-making suppliers. You can also use things like skeleton leaves and pieces of netting. Build up a selection of different textures to use.

7 FINISHING TOOLS

A rubber blending tool, available from pmc suppliers, is used to smooth the clay and for joining pieces of clay together. A paintbrush is useful for applying slip and for smoothing the clay. When the clay is dry, small needle files and sandpaper are used to shape and refine the clay.

8 FIRING EQUIPMENT

For small projects, you can use a small hand-held butane blowtorch and heat-protective mat, available from pmc suppliers and catering companies. A fire brick is another alternative. If you are doing a lot of work in pmc, it is worth buying a kiln (*right*). A pair of metal tweezers is also useful for picking up hot pieces.

9 POLISHING EQUIPMENT

A wire bristle brush (available from pmc suppliers) is the simplest way of polishing; I have also used a suede brush. A barrel polisher (*above*)—a rotating drum with steel shot inside of different shapes, with a small amount of water and tumbling soap, which inhibits rust from the steel shot—can be bought from jewellery suppliers. Alternatively, use a hobby drill with polishing attachments. A barrel polisher produces a much shinier finish than a wire brush.

10 OTHER USEFUL TOOLS

To make molds, you will need a two-part silicone rubber pack. Use a rubber block to protect your fingers when polishing with a wire brush. A hairdryer can help speed up drying times, and round- and flat-nose pliers are useful for attaching findings.

WORKING WITH PMC

Just like any other kind of clay, pmc can be rolled out and cut or molded into shape. It can then be dried, fired, and polished so that you end up with a shiny piece of silver jewellery. The exact order of working, and the detailing of each piece, will differ slightly from one project to another, but the same general principles apply. Here are some useful tips to bear in mind.

ROLLING OUT

To prevent the clay from sticking, it's a good idea to roll the clay around in your hands for 30 seconds when you first take it out of the packet. You should also rub badger balm lightly on your hands and tools.

It's important to keep the clay an even thickness when rolling it out. To do this, place playing cards ("spacers") on either side of the roller.

When you are rolling out the clay, treat it like pastry dough and turn it a few times to stop it from sticking to the board.

Put any clay that you are not using back into the packet and seal the bag to prevent it from drying out.

If the clay sticks to the board when you have finished working with it, leave it there; it will come off easily when it has dried.

Clean the workboard and roller each time you use them, to prevent dirt from being rolled into the clay the next time you work.

APPLYING TEXTURES

Put badger balm on the textured rubber mat to prevent the clay from sticking, particularly if it is a complex, deep pattern. Alternatively, apply badger balm on top of the rolled-out clay.

With some textural elements, such as leaves or feathers, it is better to place them on top of the rolled-out clay than underneath, because it is easier to remove them from the surface.

CUTTING OUT

If you want to repeat a shape many times, make a template in plastic or acetate to cut around.

Apply badger balm to the inside of your chosen cutters to prevent the clay from sticking.

JOINING PIECES OF PMC TOGETHER

Use the tip of a rubber blending tool to roughen the wet clay surfaces to be joined before you apply the slip to provide a "key."

If you are assembling many pieces, it is better to let them all dry out and sand them before joining them together with slip.

Using a rubber blending tool can be a more precise way to put the slip into joins than a paintbrush.

MAKING YOUR OWN SLIP

Grind dried-out clay to a powder in a mortar with a pestle (*below*). Put the dust into a slip pot, and add a little water to reconstitute it.

MOLD MAKING

The rubber silicone that is used to make molds comes in a two-part pack, each part being a different colour (see picture on page 10). To make a mold, mix together equal amounts of the two colours. You need to mix enough to put your object in.

Make sure the two colours of silicone are well mixed so that they merge completely, otherwise the silicone won't harden properly.

Store unmixed silicone in a cool, dark place to prevent it from going off.

Flat-backed objects such as buttons (without a shank), medals, and coins are the easiest things to use for making molds. The full process is described in the Pig Cufflink project on page 70.

To make an object without a flat back, you need to make a two-part mold. Make the first half of the mold as described in the Pig Cufflink project and leave the silicone to dry, which takes around 15 minutes. Then, instead of taking the object out of the mold, build up another layer of silicone on top and cover the top half of the object. Leave the silicone to dry, then separate the two halves and remove the object. Then make the two halves of the piece separately in the two molds (*above*) and, when dry, join them together with slip.

To check if the silicone has hardened, dig your fingernail into an unimportant part of the mold. If the mark remains visible, then the silicone has not hardened enough.

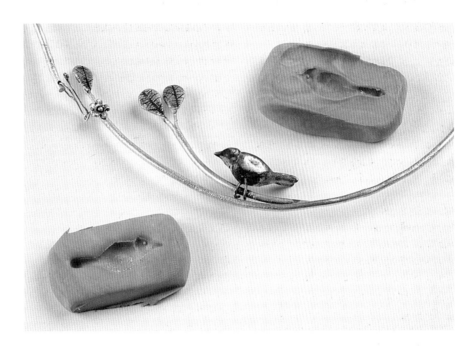

DRYING

Place a damp cloth over the clay to prevent it from drying it out while you are working on it. However, the pmc must be completely dry before it is fired. You can use a hairdryer to speed up the drying process.

FINISHING AND POLISHING

Fill any cracks or imperfections in the clay with slip or syringe, and sand them down when dry.

Instead of using a wire brush or barrel polisher, you could use polishing attachments in a hobby drill. Wear safety goggles when using the wire-brush attachments, as the wires can fly out.

When polishing with a wire brush, keep the brush going in the same direction as much as possible to get the best finish.

When using a wire brush for polishing, place the piece on a rubber block rather than holding it in your hands, as this will protect your fingers.

The tool you use for polishing depends on the finish you want to achieve: a barrel polisher produces a much shinier finish than a wire brush. To get a good finish, you need to let the barrel revolve for around an hour.

You need to clean out a barrel polisher after a few uses—and remember to add a small amount of tumbling soap each time you use it.

FIRING PMC

Precious metal clay can be fired either with a hand-held butane torch or in a kiln. Some projects can be fired by both means, and some can only be fired in a kiln. Generally speaking, larger objects and materials that require a low firing temperature, such as ceramic, glass, enamel, and some stones, can only be fired in a kiln, while smaller, simpler projects can be fired with a torch.

TORCH FIRING

The most suitable clay for torch firing is pmc3, as it requires a low firing temperature, as long as the piece isn't larger than 1 oz (25g) in weight. It is not advisable to torch fire pmc gold. You can use small catering torches that either use butane gas canisters or can be refilled with lighter fuel.

Before you fire your piece, make sure that it is bone dry. Place it on a heat-proof mat or fire brick, making sure that the firing area is free from flammable materials, and tie back your hair if it is long. Light the torch and hold it about 2 in. (5 cm) away from the piece on a medium flame. First the binder will burn away, producing a flame. Heat the pmc until it begins to glow orange. Once it

is glowing, start timing. It is important to keep the torch moving. Fire the piece for at least two minutes, and for up to five minutes for larger pieces. You can't fire something for too long, providing you don't overheat it, but you can underfire something.

Once the piece is glowing orange, you must try to keep it at this temperature.

However, if you just hold the torch directly over the piece for any length of time it will overheat and may start to melt, so you need to flick the flame on and off the piece to heat it evenly. If the piece starts to go silver in colour it is starting to melt, so remove the flame.

When you have heated the object for the correct amount of time, turn off the torch and let the piece cool down. It is then ready to polish.

KILN FIRING

There are purpose-built kilns for pmc: Evenheat and Paragon kilns are the best-known makes. These have preprogrammed settings for different types of clay. You can also program

TORCH FIRING TIMES

Type of clay	Firing time
PMC standard	The piece should glow orange for at least 5 minutes.
PMC+	The piece should glow orange for at least 10 minutes.
PMC3	The piece should glow orange for at least 2 to 5 minutes.

You can fire all three types of PMC pieces for longer than this, but not for less.

KILN FIRING TIMES

Type of clay	Temperature	Firing time
PMC standard	1652°F (900°C)	2 hours
PMC+	1652°F (900°C)	10 minutes
	1562°F (850°C)	20 minutes
	1472°F (800°C)	30 minutes
PMC3	1292°F (700°C)	10 minutes
	1202°F (650°C)	20 minutes
	1112°F (600°C)	30 minutes (for ceramics and glass)
PMC gold	1832°F (1000°C)	2 hours

in your own temperatures and times. These kilns are easy to use and turn themselves off when the program is complete. They are particularly useful if you are going to make a lot of pieces or want to do enamelling or glass fusing as well. The only negative point is the cost.

You could also use a small enamelling kiln, preferably one with a temperature regulator. These work successfully and are generally a less expensive option than the pmc kilns.

To fire your pieces in a pmc kiln, place them on a kiln shelf and not directly on the kiln floor. (You can replace the kiln shelf if it wears out.) You can also use vermiculite, which is available from garden centers, to support pieces on the kiln shelf.

HEALTH AND SAFETY

- Always be sure to fire in a well-ventilated room.
- Do not touch the sides or top of the kiln during firing.
- Do not leave the kiln or torch unattended during firing.
- Wear goggles while torch firing.
- If you have long hair, tie it up while torch firing.
- Use tweezers to pick up and move hot pmc around.
- Do not refill the torch while it is on or still hot.

SOLDERING PMC

It is possible to silver solder onto pmc, which means that you can solder on sterling-silver fittings only after the pmc has been fired. To do this, you will need traditional silver soldering equipment —a silver solder, wire cutters, tweezers, a butane torch, and safety pickle to clean the silver. A good use of soldering is to attach earring posts to the backs of stud earrings (*right*).

When silver soldering, you need to paint a flux onto the two pieces being soldered. This prevents the metal from oxidizing, which keeps it clean while it is being heated and enables the solder to flow. There are various kinds of flux, but the most common is borax, which is usually sold as a cone that can be dissolved with water.

To make flux, pour a little water into a dish and grind the borax cone into it to dissolve it. It should be the consistency of pouring cream (*below*).

Paint the flux onto the silver at the point where you want to make the join. Cut some small pieces of solder (pallions) from solder strips and dip them into the flux. Using tweezers, place the solder pieces on the join.

Light the torch. With silver soldering, it is important to heat the metal and not the solder. You must heat up the piece evenly, as it will only solder when the metal reaches the temperature at which the solder melts. There are different grades of solder and each one melts at a different temperature. If you don't want to heat a piece very much, use easy solder. If you want to solder something to a piece that is going to be enamelled, use hard solder, which will withstand the kiln temperature.

SOLDERING TEMPERATURES

Grade of solder	Melting temperature
Hard	1418°F (770°C)
Medium	1346°F (730°C)
Easy	1256°F (680°C)

When you are heating two pieces you will find the smaller object will heat up quickest. What often happens is that the solder jumps onto the hottest part, but doesn't join. The two pieces have to reach the same temperature together and then the solder will run along the join. When this happens, remove and turn off the torch.

Because pmc has a granular composition, it absorbs more solder than sterling silver. It is therefore better to use a little more solder than you would normally use in traditional silver soldering.

USING SAFETY PICKLE

After you have soldered your piece of jewellery, you need to place it in safety pickle—a warm solution of mild acid—for a few minutes until it is clean. The safety pickle removes the flux and the oxides on the sterling silver. Safety pickle only works when it is warm, but you can keep it up to temperature in a slow cooker.

When the piece is clean, remove it from the safety pickle using plastic tweezers, and wash it under running water. (Do not put steel tweezers in safety pickle, as the steel of the tweezers will cause a chemical reaction and copperplate the silver.) Your piece of jewellery is then ready for polishing.

CREATING HOLLOW FORMS

Hollow forms use less pmc, thus reducing the cost. To make a hollow pmc form you need cork or wood clay, both of which are wood reconstituted to make a type of moldable clay. This clay is used to fill the inside of the hollow form; it supports the shape of the object during firing, and will burn away during the firing process. It is very important that the cork clay is completely dry before firing, and this takes at least 24 hours. Hollow forms are best fired in a kiln; torch firing is not advisable. (It can be done, but any very thin bits of silver are liable to melt.)

Before firing completely enclosed objects, make sure that there is a very small hole to allow the air to escape—otherwise the piece may split open on the join. It is also important not to make the clay too thin or the piece may dent.

Another way of producing a hollow form is to join dried pieces of clay with slip. It is useful to make a template to get the two sides the same. Sand and shape all the pieces when they are dry, and assemble them slowly, letting the slip dry after each section. The clay is very delicate at this stage and breaks easily. Apply a lot of slip to the inside of the join, to make it stronger.

You can also use all of these techniques working with cork clay, dried pmc clay, and wet pmc clay as in the Gustav Klimt Pendant on page 122.

The title of this piece is "make a little bird house in your soul." It was made

by cutting out all the pieces that form the bird house, letting them dry and then assembling them piece by piece with slip before firing.

COMBINING PMC WITH OTHER MATERIALS

One of the advantages of pmc is that it can readily be combined with other materials, such as ceramics, glass, enamel, gold foil, and stones. You can also use it as a bezel—a surround to hold a stone in place on a piece of jewellery—or as a base for resin or polymer clay.

CERAMICS

PMC can be combined with both glazed ceramics and bisque ware (fired but unglazed clay). With glazed pieces, the pmc fuses onto the surface of the glaze. With bisque ware, it is best to paint slip onto the surface first before you apply the clay, as in the Bisque Beads on page 118. It is best to use pmc3 for any ceramic project, as it can be fired at lower temperatures than other types of pmc. This reduces the risk of the ceramic piece cracking during firing.

GLASS

The type of glass most commonly combined with pmc is dichroic glass, an iridescent glass that comes in an amazing array of colours. The best clay for the purpose is pmc3, because it can be fired at low temperatures, which reduces the risk of the glass shattering during firing. The pmc fuses onto the surface of the glass in the firing process and shrinks onto it. I have also wrapped beach glass successfully. Most glass is best fired in a kiln on a low temperature, with the pieces then being left to cool down naturally. I have also torch fired dichroic glass; it starts to melt slightly, but this can give some interesting colour and pattern effects.

ENAMEL

Enamel is the perfect partner for pmc because—unlike sterling silver—pmc does not need to be cleaned after firing. The reason for this is that pmc does not oxidize, because it is pure silver. You can use ready-made powder enamel, which you simply mix with water and paint on, or lump enamel, which has to be ground to a powder first. It is better to apply a few thin layers of enamel than one thick one.

Make sure that all the findings are in place before you enamel, as you cannot solder or drill the enamel afterwards. If you do any soldering beforehand, make sure you use enamelling or hard solder, so that it does not remelt in the kiln. You may need three or four firings to get a satisfactory finish, so it can be quite a lengthy process.

If enamel is accidentally fired onto the the silver where you don't want it, you can remove it with a carborundum stone (available from hardware stores and jewellery suppliers), which grinds off the excess enamel. You will then need to re-sand the surface of the silver to remove scratches made by the stone.

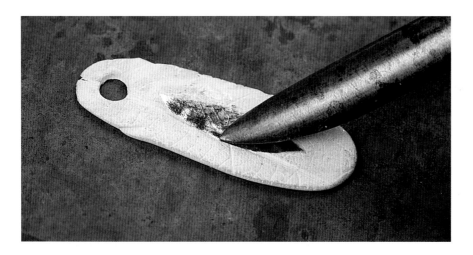

GOLD FOIL

Another great looking finish for pmc is the application of gold foil. This is actually a traditional Korean technique called keum-boo, which involves fusing 24ct gold foil onto the silver. You must use gold foil from a pmc supplier, as calligraphy gold leaf is too thin.

First, put the pmc piece on the hot plate, then heat up the hot plate. It needs to be between 1382° and 1562°F (750° and 850°C) for the gold foil to fuse with the surface of the silver. Put on some tight-fitting gardening gloves to protect your hands, as it gets very hot working so close to the hot plate. When the hot plate reaches the required temperature, gently rub a burnishing tool over the foil.

Try to avoid tearing the gold, although you can put more foil over the top if necessary. Pay particular attention to the edges of the foil, to make sure they adhere properly (*above*). If the piece overheats, the gold foil will melt and disappear into the surface.

When you have finished, let the piece cool down and then try lifting the foil up with your fingernail. If it lifts up, it has not adhered properly and you will need to repeat the burnishing process.

STONES

Certain stones can be fired directly in place. The most commonly used are cubic zirconias, which are man-made, faceted stones. The advantages of using them are that they withstand high temperatures in firing and they come in a wide range of shapes and colours.

Other stones that can be fired with pmc are diamonds, sapphires, and rubies, which can all be fired at quite high temperatures. Another advantage of sapphires and rubies is that they can be bought as cabochons, which means they are flat bottomed and have a domed top, and are not sparkly like cut stones. I have also used garnets, which are much less expensive than the other natural stones. I have also seen quartz-based stones used, but they are more likely to crack along fault lines. As a general rule, man-made stones require a high temperature setting in the kiln, while natural stones are better at a low temperature.

SETTING STONES

This section gives you some tips on setting stones into pmc. The benefit of pmc is that it is as easy to set a square stone as it is to set a round one, which is not the case with traditional jewellery-making techniques.

SETTING FACETED STONES

Faceted or cut stones, either man made or natural, have a pointed bottom to them and come up to the girth, which is the widest part of the stone. There are many different cuts and shapes.

Always make a tiny hole with a pin in the pmc into which you're setting the stone, under the point of the stone. This allows any air to escape from underneath (trapped air can sometimes push the stone out). If you wish, you can make the hole underneath the stone larger to allow light to shine through the stone; this is particularly effective in a pair of earrings, where you see through both sides.

When you build up the setting for the stone you must make sure that the clay comes up over the girth. This is to allow for the clay shrinking back during the firing; if the clay shrinks back to below the girth, the stone may fall out.

When the clay has dried, you can sand it and refine it to neaten the setting. Make sure, however, that there is no clay on the front of the stone before you fire it, otherwise the clay will be fired onto the front of the stone and the appearance of your piece of jewellery will be ruined.

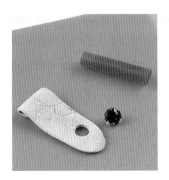

1 To make a hidden setting, make a hole in the clay slightly smaller than the stone with a skewer or the tip of a round needle file.

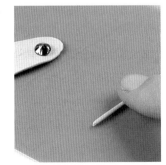

2 When the clay is dry, place the stone behind the hole on the back of the piece. Roll out a thin ring of clay to go around the base of the stone.

3 Attach the ring of clay to the back of the piece with slip. This traps the stone on the back of the piece of jewellery. It can then be fired in place.

SETTING CABOCHON STONES

Provided they will withstand the firing, you can also set cabochon stones into pmc. The higher the stones are on the Moes scale of hardness, the more likely they will be to survive firing—so sapphires, rubies, obsidian, and sunstone are all stones that will work. Alternatively, you can fire a setting into the pmc and set the stone after firing, which gives you a wider choice of stones to use.

The benefit of cabochon stones is they are flat bottomed, which makes them easier to position. As with setting faceted stones, make a small ring of clay to enclose the stone and attach it to your piece of jewellery with slip.

SETTING STONES AFTER FIRING

For stones that are going to be set after firing, a different process is required, which involves some traditional jewellery-making techniques. If you already make jewellery, you can make a setting to fit your stone out of fine silver bezel strip. Solder it with hard solder, embed it into position on your pmc piece, and fire it in place. Because the setting is not made from pmc it does not shrink during firing, so you can set your stone afterwards using a bezel pusher and burnisher.

If you do not want to solder a setting, a number of companies now make fine silver settings in different shapes that can be embedded into the pmc and fired.

PATINATING PMC

Patination, which gives the piece an antique look, can be done using either liver of sulphur or Platinol. Patination should be done after polishing.

To mix up liver of sulphur, put some hot water in a glass jar and add a small amount of liver of sulphur. The weaker the solution, the more subtle the colours; if the solution goes yellow, it is too strong and will turn the silver completely black. Make sure you read the health and safety instructions on the packaging. Do not mix up too much liver of sulphur at a time as it does not have a very long shelf life.

Hold the piece of jewellery under hot running water before putting it in the solution with a pair of plastic tweezers. Watch the colour: it should go from yellows and bronzes through to blues and black.

When you like the colour, use tweezers to take the jewellery out of the solution and hold it under cold running water.

It is easier to use Platinol, although the range of colours that you can create is smaller than that achieved using liver of sulphur. You can paint on Platinol directly from the bottle or dilute it with water for a lighter finish. Platinol is used cold and keeps for longer than liver of sulphur.

WIREWORK TECHNIQUES

The majority of the projects in this book can be completed without using any of the traditional jewellery-making techniques such as silver soldering. However, you still need to learn how to attach ready-made clasps to your pieces of jewellery—and it's useful to be able to form wire into decorative shapes, such as spirals. All you need are a couple of pairs of pliers and some silver or silver-plated wire.

DECORATIVE SPIRALS

Spirals can be used as decoration on earrings and necklaces as in the Turquoise Necklace on page 44, or impressed into clay to form a pattern, as in the Gustav Klimt pendant on page 122.

TOOLS AND MATERIALS
6 in. (15 cm) 24-gauge (0.6mm) silver-plated wire
round-nose pliers
flat-nose pliers

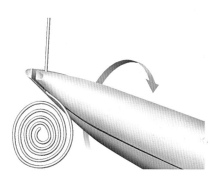

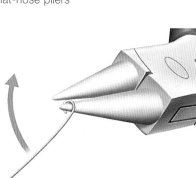

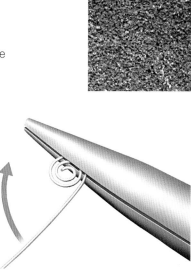

1 Using the tip of the round-nose pliers, make a tiny loop at the end of the wire.

2 Hold the loop in the flat-nose pliers, holding the wire firmly but not so tightly that the pliers leave their mark. Using your finger and thumb, wind the wire around the first loop so that a coil begins to develop. Open the pliers to reposition the coil as you work.

3 When the spiral is the desired size, use flat-nose pliers to bend the wire away from the spiral at an angle of 90 degrees.

CLOSED LOOP

A closed loop is the most secure way to hang a bead or charm, as in the Little Mermaid on page 52, or to link a chain. This is the most important and versatile technique in all wirework and deserves to be practised.

TOOLS AND MATERIALS

5 in. (12 cm) 24-gauge (0.6mm) silver-
  plated wire
round-nose pliers
flat-nose pliers
wire cutters
beads

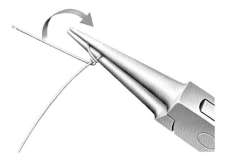

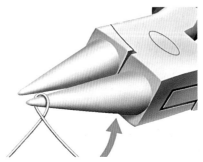

1 Use the tip of the round-nose pliers to form a "bow" shape about 1¼ in. (3 cm) from one end of the wire.

2 Hold the loop of the bow sideways in the pliers so that the longer end of the wire points straight out from the loop. Bend the shorter length of wire so that it is at right angles to the longer length. Holding the loop firmly in the pliers, use your finger and thumb to wrap the shorter length of wire under and over the longer one, as shown. Repeat this two or three times, keeping the wraps neat and close together.

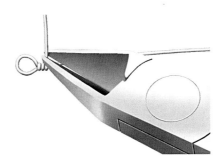

3 After the last wrap, cut off the end of the wrapping wire with the wire cutters, cutting in as close as possible.

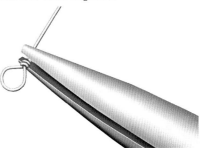

4 Use the flat-nose pliers to press the end of the cut wire back against the wraps. You have made a closed loop.

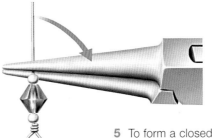

5 To form a closed loop above beads, place the round-nose pliers against the bead to create a space similar in size to that filled by the wraps by your first closed loop. Bend the wire towards you at an angle of 90 degrees, making sure you don't lose the space marked by the pliers.

6 Change the angle of the round-nose pliers so they are almost vertical to the beads. Roll the wire over the pliers to create another loop above the space.

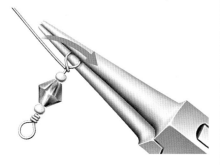

7 Hold this loop in the flat-nose pliers and wrap the loose wire back towards the bead with your finger and thumb. Try to match the size of the original closed loop.

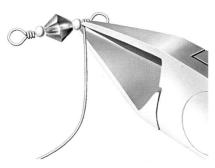

8 Cut off the excess wire and press in the end, as you did in Steps 3 and 4.

WIRING TO HANG

This technique is an extension of the closed loop. Use it when you want a button or bead to lie flat when suspended on a chain or cord.

TOOLS AND MATERIALS

5 in. (12 cm) 24-gauge (0.6mm)
   silver-plated wire
bead or two-hole button
round-nose pliers
flat-nose pliers
wire cutters

1 Thread the wire through a hole in the button or bead that you want to hang. Fold the wire about 1¹/₂ in. (4 cm) along.

2 Wrap the shorter end of the wire around the longer length several times with your finger and thumb, then finish the loop as you did in Steps 3 and 4 of making a Closed Loop.

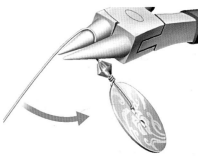

3 Add a bead above these wraps and make another closed loop. This loop should be sideways on to your hanging piece, so adjust the angle of the pliers before you begin. Make sure that the loop is large enough for your chosen cord or chain; you can make it larger by wrapping the wire around a wider part of the shaft of the pliers.

CRIMPING

This technique is used to attach a fastener to a necklace or a bracelet, as in the Daisy Necklace on page 26, or to group sections of buttons or beads onto a cord or wire. To secure small groups of buttons or beads, thread a crimp bead onto the wire or cord and squeeze it into position with pliers. Crimping pliers are specially designed for the task, but you can use flat-nose, or even round-nose, pliers if you wish.

in the Daisy Necklace on page 26

TOOLS AND MATERIALS
clasp
crimp beads
crimping or flat-nose pliers

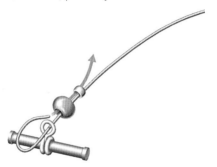

1 To attach a fastener, position a crimp bead on the wire or cord. Thread the wire through one end of the clasp, then back through the crimp bead.

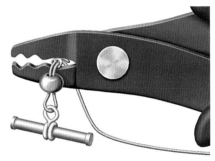

2 Place the crimp bead close enough to the clasp to make a neat loop. Squeeze the crimp bead flat with crimping or flat-nose pliers, then cut off any excess wire or cord.

DESIGNING JEWELLERY

When you're faced with a blank piece of paper or a ball of clay, the idea of designing a piece of jewellery can be quite daunting. Looking at other pieces of jewellery is a good place to start, as you can find out what styles you like and what is in fashion— although ultimately it can be difficult not to simply copy what you see. To design a piece that is truly your own, it is better to look at other objects such as flowers, sculpture, or shells. Inspiration can come from unexpected places. A lot of my own work, for example, is derived from song lyrics or poetry. There are three basic approaches to designing—taking a particular process or technique (not necessariy one associated with jewellery making) as your starting point, using an object or image as a visual stimulus, and creating a design that conveys a specific idea or message.

DESIGNING USING A PROCESS

This involves using a particular process or technique as the main theme of the piece of jewellery and showing it off to its best effect. For example, I made a range of jewellery based on sewing techniques—such as cross stitch and weaving—and translated it into metal, using wire as the "thread" (*left*).

DESIGNING USING AN OBJECT OR IMAGE

This approach involves taking something that interests you—perhaps a painting, a sculpture, a piece of ceramics or glassware, or flowers and leaves—and using it as the visual stimulus for your own design. You might, for example, echo the shape or the texture in your piece; alternatively, you might try to capture the overall impression in your jewellery piece or even take just one element from a large piece and use it as the basis for your design. A good example of this approach is the Gustav Klimt Pendant on page 122. I made the textures and colours the most important feature of the design, but you might see something different.

DESIGNING FOR PMC

To design well for pmc, you must take its properties into account. Because of its composition, pmc is weaker than sterling silver, so avoid making any long thin parts that are unsupported. Use it for its moldable qualities and the fact that you can apply textures easily.

DESIGNING TO CONVEY AN IDEA

The intention of this way of designing is to convey an idea, sentiment, belief, or story within a piece of jewellery. There is often an accompanying narrative to describe it. A jeweller who does this very well is Mah Rana, a well-known international jeweller who has had many exhibitions. My example is the bird in the cage necklace (*above*); the song title "Born To Be Wild" is inscribed on the bar above it.

It is also worth thinking about any fittings that you might need, so you can incorporate them into the design from the outset, rather than their being an afterthought. The example below shows four different ways of attaching a chain to a pendant; think about which would be appropriate and sympathetic to your design.

DESIGNING WITH POLYMER CLAY

Something that both I and my students have found useful is to design a piece of jewellery first in polymer clay. This allows you to experiment with your ideas and avoid costly mistakes. It is also useful if you find it difficult to draw a design.

Most of what you can do with polymer clay can be done with pmc. The difference is that polymer clay does not dry out while you are working with it. Once you have designed your piece in polymer clay, make sure that you clean all your tools thoroughly and remove any polymer clay so that it does not get mixed in with the pmc, which could ruin your final piece.

CHAPTER 1

ROLLING OUT

D A I S Y
NECKLACE

MATERIALS
small packet pmc3 clay
2 x 5mm silver jump rings
17 in. (44 cm) tigertail wire
4 freshwater pearls
12 rose quartz chips
2 silver crimp beads
1 x 5mm silver bolt ring

TOOLS
badger balm
roller and spacers
workboard
skeleton leaf or texture plate
1-in. (2.5-cm) circle cutter
1/2-in. (13mm) daisy cutter
1 bugle bead to make the holes
sandpaper
round needle file
butane torch and heatproof mat
  or fire brick, or kiln
wire brush and rubber block,
  or barrel polisher
flat-nose pliers

The Daisy Necklace is a good first project as it allows you to practise the basic skills of rolling, cutting, and texturing that will be used in many other projects in the book. I created the delicate flower necklace using dainty freshwater pearls and gemstone chips, but there are many variations you can make. Other complementary beads, such as amber and tiger's eye, or garnet and white pearl, would create a completely different effect. Simply choose a combination that suits you. This design can also work with a heart or a star shape. You can use the same cutter to make a pair of matching earrings from leftover clay to wear with the necklace. For a totally different look, swap the tigertail wire for a ribbon and omit the beads.

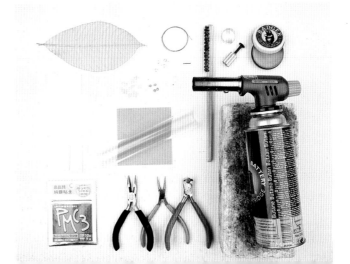

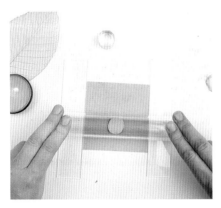

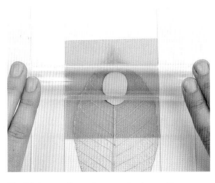

1 Rub badger balm on your tools and hands to prevent the clay from sticking, then roll out a piece of clay on the workboard to a thickness of about 1/16 in. (1 or 2mm). (Put the rest of the clay back in the packet to prevent it from drying out.) Measure the rolled-out piece against the circle cutter to make sure it is the right size.

2 Pick up the clay and place the skeleton leaf or texture plate on the board. Place the clay back down on top of it and roll over it gently with the roller. Turn the clay over and peel off the leaf.

3 With the clay textured side up, cut out a circle with the circle cutter. Gently remove the excess clay and put it back in the packet to prevent it from drying out.

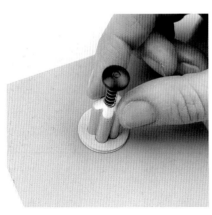

4 Place the daisy cutter in the middle of the circle and push down firmly.

5 Gently remove the cutter. If the daisy shape does not come away (as shown here), leave both pieces to dry where they are before you attempt to separate them.

6 Before the pieces dry, make holes in them with the bugle bead. Pierce one hole at the top of the circle and one at the bottom about 1/16 in. (1 or 2mm) from the edge. Make another hole in one of the petals of the daisy. Don't worry if the bugle bead holes do not come out cleanly, as you can clean up the holes when the pieces are dry.

7 The pieces must be completely dry before firing. (You can speed up the process by using a hairdryer.) Once they are dry, carefully remove the two shapes from the board and gently sand the edges.

8 Clean up the holes with a round needle file.

9 The pieces are now ready to fire, either in a kiln or with a butane torch on a heatproof mat or fire brick (see page 12).

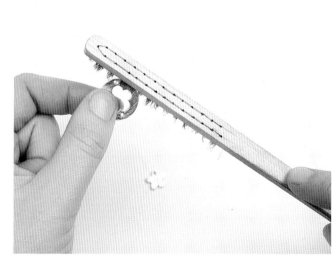 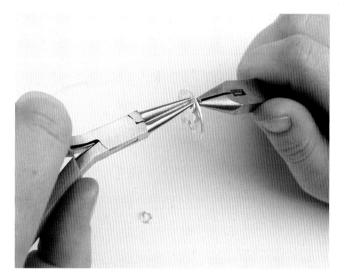

10 Once fired, let the pieces cool down, then polish them with a wire brush or in a barrel polisher (see page 11). Textures come out very well with a wire brush, whereas a barrel polisher will result in a shinier finish.

11 Now make the pieces into a necklace. Take a 5mm silver jump ring, open it up with flat-nose pliers, and link it through the bottom hole in the circle.

12 Link the daisy onto the jump ring and, using the flat-nose pliers, close the jump ring tightly to connect the daisy and circle together. Link a second jump ring through the top hole in the circle.

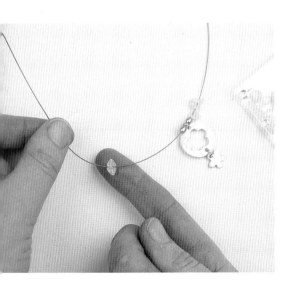

13 Thread the length of tigertail wire through the top jump ring, then thread on the beads. Slide a silver crimp bead over one end of the tigertail wire. Loop the end of the wire back down through the crimp bead, leaving a loop of wire protruding beyond the crimp bead. Using flat-nose pliers, squeeze the crimp bead flat to secure it on the wire. Repeat at the other end of the wire, and trim off the excess wire.

14 To complete the necklace, attach a silver bolt ring to one end of the tigertail wire using flat-nose pliers.

VARIATION

*If you have some leftover clay,
why not make a pair of matching
earrings? Remember to make a
hole in one petal of each earring so
that you can insert the ear wires.*

H E A R T
BUTTONS

MATERIALS
small packet pmc3 clay

TOOLS
badger balm
roller and spacers
workboard
texture plate
cutter
1 bugle bead to make the holes
sandpaper
round needle file
butane torch and heatproof mat
  or fire brick, or kiln
wire brush and rubber block,
  or barrel polisher
sewing needle and thread

This is one of the simplest projects for pmc, and can transform a plain garment into something really stylish. Buttons also make fantastic embellishments for all kinds of craft projects. If you are replacing buttons on clothes, make sure that the diameter of the cutter you are using is larger than the old button, as the clay will shrink by about 10 percent in firing. A set of buttons makes a great and unique present.

1 Rub a small amount of badger balm on your tools and hands, then roll out the clay on the workboard, using three playing cards on each side as spacers to keep the clay an even thickness. (If you want the button to be thicker, put more playing cards on each side.) Pick up the clay and lay it down on the texture plate that you have chosen. Gently roll over the clay, then peel it off the texture plate and lay it back down, pattern side up. Using your chosen cutter, cut out the required number of buttons.

2 Peel away the excess clay from around the cut-out shapes and put it back in the packet to prevent it from drying out.

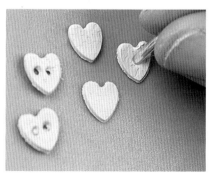

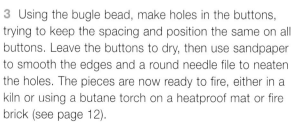

3 Using the bugle bead, make holes in the buttons, trying to keep the spacing and position the same on all buttons. Leave the buttons to dry, then use sandpaper to smooth the edges and a round needle file to neaten the holes. The pieces are now ready to fire, either in a kiln or using a butane torch on a heatproof mat or fire brick (see page 12).

4 Once fired, let the pieces cool down, then polish them with a wire brush or in a barrel polisher (see page 11).

5 Sew the buttons in place. I used a contrasting colour of thread as a design feature.

P E T
TAG

MATERIALS
small packet pmc3 clay
Platinol
5mm decorative eyelets
1 x 8mm large jump ring

TOOLS
badger balm
workboard
roller and spacers
letter stamps
cutter
round needle file
sandpaper
butane torch and heatproof mat
  or fire brick, or kiln
wire brush and rubber block,
  or barrel polisher
eyelet tool
hammer
flat-nose pliers

Make a special tag, stamped with your pet's name, to attach to their collar. You could also add your phone number so that people can contact you if your pet strays.

There are a number of different letter stamps that you can use. The ones that I use are from a silversmithing company, but you can find ones that are used in card making that work just as well as long as the scale is right.

The size and shape of the tag is determined by the number of letters in your pet's name. Sort out the letter stamps that you are going to use and lay them out ready before you start the project.

For a pretty finishing touch I added decorative eyelets, which are usually used in card making. It is always interesting to look at other crafts to see what materials and tools can cross over.

1 Rub badger balm on your tools and hands, and roll out the clay to about 1/16 in. (1 or 2mm) thick. Stamp your pet's name on the surface of the clay, making sure you do not press all the way through. (Practise on polymer clay first, to make sure that the cutter you have chosen is big enough to contain the name.)

2 Press the cutter firmly into the clay to cut out the tag, making sure you centre the name within the shape. (Alternatively, you could cut a shape using a craft knife and template.) Gently remove the excess clay and put it back in the packet to prevent it from drying out.

3 Place an eyelet at the point from which you want the tag to hang, making sure that it is not too close to the edge. Press it down firmly to push out a little circle of clay.

4 Using a round needle file or a piece of wire, enlarge the hole to allow for shrinkage when the piece is fired. Leave the tag to dry. When it is dry, sand the edges and enlarge the hole again with the round needle file. The pieces are now ready to fire, either in a kiln or with a butane torch on a heatproof mat or fire brick (see page 12). Once fired, let the piece cool down, then polish with a wire brush or in a barrel polisher (see page 11).

5 To make the letters show up more clearly, patinate areas of the tag with a cold solution of Platinol, painting the Platinol directly onto the silver, as shown. Alternatively, dip the tag into the solution; when it comes out, the whole piece will be darkened (see page 18). Leave to dry.

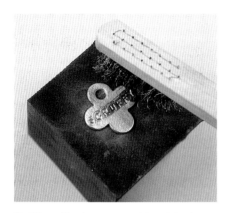

6 Place the tag on a rubber block. Using a wire brush, polish the raised areas and leave the indents dark. (Alternatively, you could polish the whole piece in a barrel polisher; see page 11.)

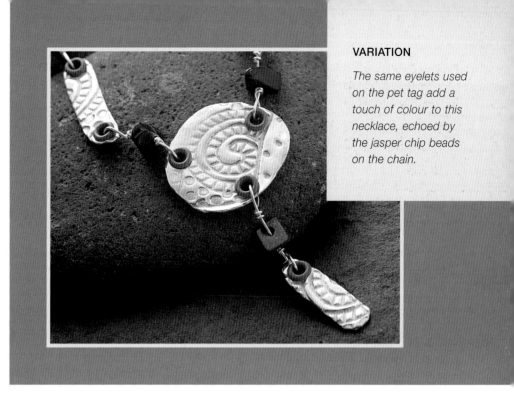

VARIATION

The same eyelets used on the pet tag add a touch of colour to this necklace, echoed by the jasper chip beads on the chain.

7 Push an eyelet through the hole in the tag. (If the hole is not big enough, enlarge it with a round needle file.) Turn the tag over.

8 Place the eyelet tool on the back of the eyelet and hit with a hammer until the edges of the eyelet are turned over and secure.

9 Using flat-nose pliers, open up a large jump ring. Link it through the eyelet and the name-tag loop on your pet's collar, and use the pliers to close the jump ring securely.

S T A R
STUDS

MATERIALS
scraps of pmc3 clay
pmc3 slip

If soldering:
2 x silver ear posts with
  butterfly studs
medium syringe silver solder
borax

If gluing:
2 x silver ear posts with flat
  bases
quick-drying epoxy adhesive

TOOLS
badger balm
workboard
roller and spacers
small star cutter
small daisy cutter
sandpaper
paintbrush
butane torch and heatproof
  mat or fire brick, or kiln
wire brush and rubber
  block, or barrel polisher

If soldering:
paintbrush
reverse-action tweezers
plastic tweezers
safety pickle

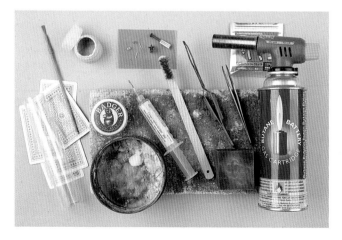

Use up leftover scraps of clay to make a little pair of studs, perfect for wearing every day.

The most secure method of attaching the stars is to silver solder them to the posts. You can use traditional solder, but I find syringe solder is ideal. Alternatively, use ear posts with a flat base, glue them to the backs of the stars, and leave them to dry. This is not the strongest method, however, and the posts are likely to come off with a lot of wear.

1 Rub badger balm on your tools and hands, then roll out a piece of clay on the workboard to a thickness of about 1/16 in. (1 or 2mm). Using the cutters, cut out two stars and two daisies. Remove the excess clay from around the shapes and put it back in the packet to prevent it from drying out. Leave the pieces to dry, then sand the edges with sandpaper. Pick up each daisy in turn and paint some pmc3 slip onto the back.

2 Place each daisy in the middle of a star and leave to dry again. The pieces are now ready to fire, with a butane torch on a heatproof mat or fire brick (see page 12). Once fired, let the pieces cool down, then polish them with a wire brush or in a barrel polisher (see page 11).

3 If you are soldering the posts to the earrings, mix some borax flux (see page 13), paint some onto the back of the stars, and place them on a heatproof mat or fire brick. Paint some flux onto the end of the earring posts and, using reverse-action tweezers, place one post in the centre of the back of each star, so that they stand upright. Squeeze a small amount of medium syringe solder onto the base of the earring posts, so that it touches both the posts and the earring base. Solder the posts to the earring bases. Allow to cool, then place in safety pickle (see page 14) for a few minutes.

4 Polish the earrings either in a barrel polisher or using a wire brush (see page 11). Push the butterfly studs onto the posts.

R O B O T
PIN

MATERIALS
large packet pmc3 clay
pmc3 slip
pmc3 syringe
large safety pin

2 x 6mm silver jump rings or
  6mm split pins
2 x 15mm glass hearts

TOOLS
badger balm
workboard
roller and spacers
sequin waste
3/4-in. (2-cm) square cutter
1/2-in. (13-mm) square cutter
1/4-in. (6-mm) circle cutter
1/4-in. (6-mm) heart cutter
pen

sandpaper
flat needle file
craft knife
paintbrush
butane torch and heatproof
  mat or fire brick, or kiln
wire brush and rubber
  block, or barrel polisher
rubber block

This is a quirky piece of jewellery, made using standard-sized cutters. Experiment with different cutters to see what other creatures you can create, practising first with polymer clay. I attached my robot to a large safety pin, but he could be hung on a pendant. He looks great holding a chunky cardigan together.

1 Rub badger balm on your tools and hands, then roll out a piece of clay on the board to a thickness of about 1/16 in. (1 or 2mm). Place the sequin waste on top of the clay, gently roll over the top, then peel off the sequin waste. Using the cutters, cut out a large (3/4-in./2-cm) and a medium (1/2-in./13-mm) square. Using the tip of a pen, make indents around the edge of the large square. Leave both squares to dry.

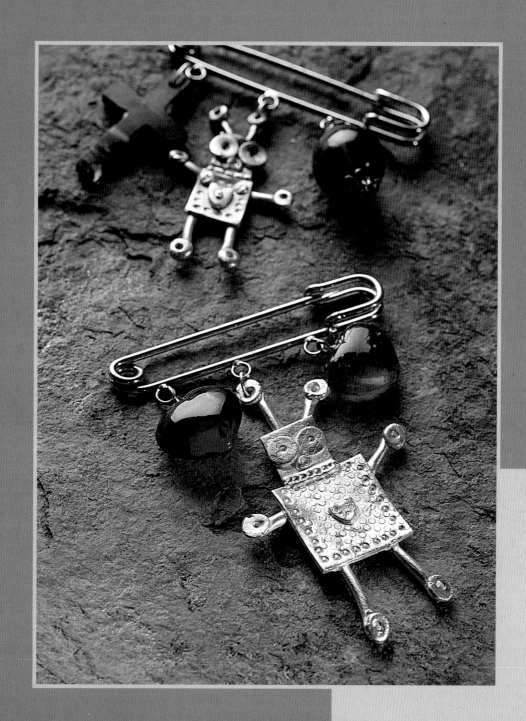

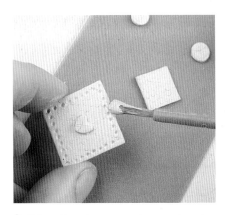

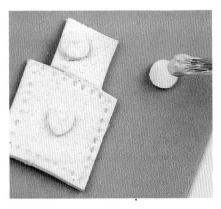

2 Reroll the excess clay. You can texture it with another geometric pattern if you wish. Using the cutters, cut out two circles and one heart. Using the pen tip again, make a dot in the middle of each circle for the middle of the robot's eyes. Leave to dry.

3 When the pieces are dry, sand and file the edges. To join them together, paint some slip on the back of the heart and place it in the centre of the large square. Paint slip along the top edge of the large square, then centre the medium square along this edge to form the robot's head.

4 Paint slip on the back of the circles, then place the circles on the medium square to make the robot's eyes.

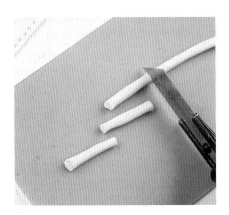

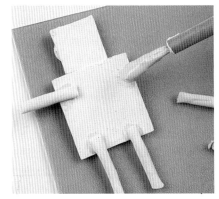

5 Roll a small piece of clay into a long, thin sausage shape and, using a craft knife, cut six short pieces about 1/2 in. (13mm) long.

6 Turn the robot's head and body over. Dab a little slip onto the base of the body and carefully press on two lengths of clay to create the robot's legs. Repeat on the sides of the body and on the top of the head to form the arms and antennae.

7 When the figure has dried a little, turn it back over. Take a little more clay and roll up little balls. Paint a little slip onto the bottom of the robot's legs and press one ball onto the base of each leg to make the feet.

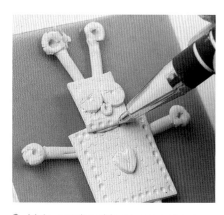

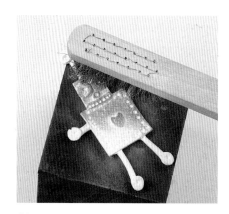

8 Using the end of the pen, make an indentation in the middle of each foot. Now do the same for the hands and the top of the antennae, but in the antennae poke holes all the way through. Make one tiny ball and, using slip, stick it below the eyes to make the nose

9 Make another thin sausage shape, stick it over the join between the head and the body with slip, press in some tiny indentations, and trim off the excess at the edges. There are many different details you could make to create a small robot family!

10 Leave the figure to dry, then sand any untidy edges and fill any cracks with slip or syringe. The robot is now ready to fire, either in a kiln or with a butane torch on a heatproof mat or fire brick (see page 12). Once fired, let the piece cool down, then polish with a wire brush for a satin finish (see page 11).

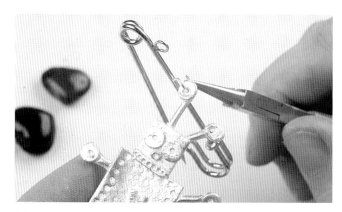

11 Using flat-nose pliers, open two jump rings. Link the jump rings first into the holes in the antennae and then into the loop on the safety pin, and close up the jump rings securely. Attach two glass heart-shaped beads in the same way.

T U R Q U O I S E
NECKLACE

MATERIALS

small packet pmc3 clay
1 bugle bead
18 in. (45 cm) 7-strand tigertail wire
6 small silver crimp beads
21 turquoise chips
8 in. (20 cm) 24-gauge (0.6mm)
   silver wire

TOOLS

badger balm
workboard
roller and spacers
rubber texture plate
1½-in. (4-cm) star cutter
round needle file
sandpaper
butane torch and heatproof mat
   or fire brick
wire brush and rubber block,
   or barrel polisher
scissors
flat-nose pliers
round-nose pliers
wire cutters

This project is a good example of how a simple design using easy techniques can result in a very effective piece of jewellery. The technique works very well with other cut-out shapes, such as flowers and hearts. I chose turquoise chips for this necklace, as this stone helps create a bold design. Equally, you could choose chipstones with a softer colour, such as amethysts or peridots. Changing the texture background will also alter the look of the piece.

The cut-out shape made in Step 5 can be used in another project, or simply made into a smaller pendant. Make sure you pierce a hole in it before it dries, so that you can hang it later

1 Rub badger balm on your tools and hands to prevent the clay from sticking. Take a lump of clay and put the rest back in the packet to prevent it from drying out.

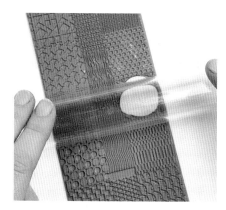

2 Roll the clay into a ball with your hands, then flatten it out on the workboard so that it makes a neat, circular shape. Roll it out on the board to a thickness of about 1/16 in. (1 or 2mm). Place the clay on a rubber texture plate and gently roll over the top of it.

3 Carefully peel the clay away from the texture plate to check the result. If you're not happy with the texture, redo it. (In this design I left the edges as they were and did not try to neaten them up.)

4 Place the star cutter in the middle of the rolled-out clay and push down.

5 The central star should come away. (This piece is not used in the project, so put the clay back in the packet, or use the star shape to make an earring or a brooch.)

6 While the clay is still damp, use the bugle bead to pierce two holes at the top and three along the bottom of the outer rim. Don't worry if the holes aren't perfect as you can clean them up later. Leave the piece to dry.

7 Clean up the holes using a round needle file. Use a piece of sandpaper to go around the inside of the star. Leave the edges of the pendant rough.

8 The star is now ready to fire in a kiln or with a butane torch on a heatproof mat or fire brick (see page 12).

9 Polish the fired star with a wire brush or in a barrel polisher (see page 11).

10 Once the star is polished, cut the tigertail wire in half with scissors and slide a crimp bead onto one end. Thread one piece of tigertail wire through one of the holes at the top of the pendant, then loop the tigertail wire back through the crimp bead. Flatten the crimp bead with flat-nose pliers to secure it. Repeat on the other side of the star.

11 Thread three turquoise chips onto the tigertail wire, then slide another crimp bead onto the wire and crimp it about 1 1/2 in. (4 cm) above the last turquoise chip (see page 22).

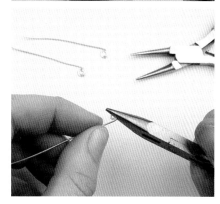

12 Thread on three more turquoise chips, then secure with another crimp bead. Repeat on the other side. Open up the bolt ring with the flat-nose pliers, attach it to the right-hand side loop, and close securely.

13 Using wire cutters, cut three pieces of 24-gauge (0.6mm) silver wire about 2 in. (5 cm) long. (You can trim them down later if you find they're too long.) At one end of each piece of wire, using round-nose pliers, form a loop. Hold the loop in flat-nose pliers and bend the wire around in a spiral (see page 19), leaving 1 1/4 in. (3 cm) of wire bare.

14 Thread three turquoise chips onto each piece of wire. Thread the first length of wire through one of the holes at the bottom of the pendant and, using round-nose pliers, form the end into a closed loop (see page 20). Wind the excess wire around the long length and trim off any leftover wire. Repeat with the other two lengths of wire.

F L O W E R
PIN

MATERIALS
pmc3 clay
pmc3 slip
6 in. (15 cm) 20-gauge (0.8mm)
  silver wire
21 green seed beads
pin protector

TOOLS
badger balm
workboard
roller and spacers
texture plate
rubber blending tool
craft knife
skewer
paintbrush
sandpaper
butane torch and heatproof mat
  or fire brick, or kiln
wire brush and rubber block,
  or barrel polisher
wire cutters
flat-nose pliers
round-nose pliers
steel stake
flat metal hammer
needle file

This is quite a traditional design that can be used as a lapel pin or a hat pin. I've always loved making these roses in different materials; you could also try different types of flowers, such as arum lilies or fuchsias.

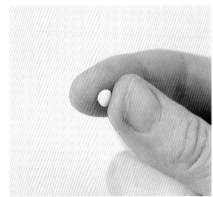

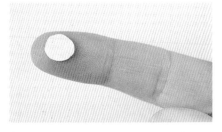

1 To make the flowers, I use a cake-decorating technique. Take a very small ball of clay and squash it flat between your fingers.

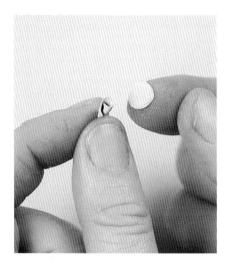

2 Curl it around itself to create the central petals of the rose. Continue making petals and join them together with a little slip, overlapping them slightly to build up the shape and making the outer petals slightly bigger. Use a rubber blending tool to smooth the petals together. You will need about ten petals for each rose.

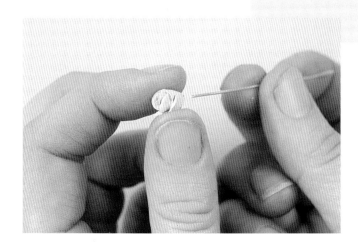

3 Take a 2-in. (5-cm) length of silver wire and push it into the end of the first rose. For the other two roses, use 1¼-in. (3-cm) lengths of wire.

4 Gently pull the petals so that the edges curl outwards. (You can practise making the roses with polymer clay.) Leave the roses to dry.

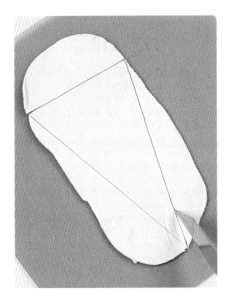

5 To make the holder for the flowers, roll out some clay about three cards thick and impress the pattern of your choice, then cut out a large triangle about 1½ in. (4 cm) across at the base and as long as you would like it. Take away the excess clay, then carefully lift the triangle off the board.

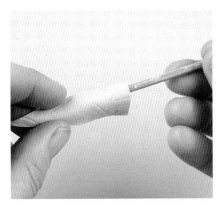

6 With the textured side facing outwards, roll the clay into a cone shape, slightly overlapping at the back. (Use a wooden skewer to help shape it.) Make sure that you leave a hole at the tip of the cone large enough to put a piece of wire through.

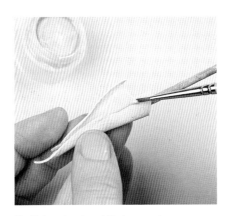

7 If the clay is a bit dry, apply some slip to the join. You can also splay out the top of the cone slightly—but make sure you leave a small gap at the tip to allow the wire to go through.

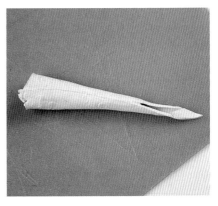

8 When you are pleased with the shape leave it to dry, then sand any edges to neaten them. The pieces are ready to fire, either in a kiln on a pmc3 fast setting or with a butane torch on a heatproof mat or fire brick (see page 12). Once fired, polish them with a wire brush or in a barrel polisher (see page 11).

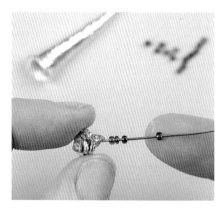

9 Thread seven green seed beads onto each of the wires in the flowers.

10 Twist the two shorter wires around the longer one, so that the flowers are joined together. Press the twisted wires with flat-nose pliers so that there are no sharp ends sticking out.

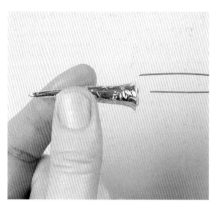

11 Cut a 4-in. (10-cm) length of silver wire and bend it in half. Push one end into the wide end of the cone, so that it pokes out of the hole at the tip

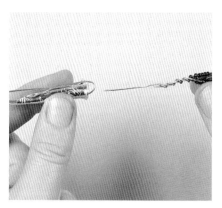

12 Insert the bunch of flowers into the cone, pushing the wire through the hole in the narrow end.

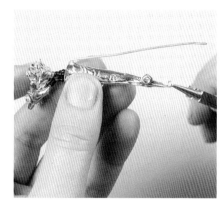

13 Using round-nose pliers, form a loop at the end of each of the two wires protruding through the narrow end of the cone. Hold each loop in turn with flat-nose pliers and bend the wire to form a spiral (see page 19), so that the wires cannot pull out.

14 The long silver wire at the wide end of the cone is going to become the pin. Using a flat needle file, file the end to a point. Place the bend in the wire on a steel stake, and hammer it with a flat metal hammer. This flattens the wire and makes it stronger. Put the pin protector on the end of the pin.

L I T T L E
MERMAID

MATERIALS
large packet pmc3 clay
pmc3 slip
pmc3 syringe
1 x 6mm silver jump ring
1 x 8mm silver jump ring
16 in. (40 cm) 1/2-in. (13mm) ribbon
1 x 15mm large pearl
1 x 8mm bell
2 in. (5 cm) 24-gauge (0.6mm)
  silver wire

TOOLS
badger balm
workboard
roller and spacers
net bag
1/2 in. (13mm) triangle cutter
1 in. (2.5 cm) teardropcutter
1/2 in. (13mm) circle cutter
1/4 in. (6mm) circle cutter
ballpoint pen
sandpaper
paintbrush
rubber blending tool
butane torch and heatproof mat
  or fire brick, or kiln
wire brush and rubber block,
  or barrel polisher
round-nose pliers
flat-nose pliers
wire cutters

This is a fun project that all little girls will love—and some bigger ones, too! You could personalize the mermaid by stamping a name on the body. Experiment with the cutters to create different characters, such as the Fairy on page 55. Practise with polymer clay to see what you can come up with.

1 Rub badger balm on your tools and hands, and roll out the clay on the workboard, using thin spacers to keep the thickness even. Put your chosen texture underneath the clay (I used a net bag to imitate fish scales), then gently roll over the top. Using the cutters, cut out one small triangle and one large teardrop shape and leave to dry.

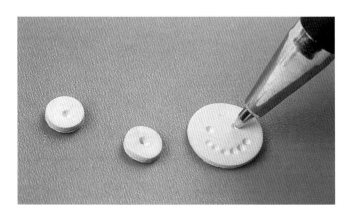

2 Reroll the excess clay and cut out one large and two small circles. Using the tip of a ballpoint pen, make a dot in the middle of each small circle. On the large circle, which is going to be the face, make a line of dots for a smile and two dots for eyes. Leave all the pieces to dry. When the pieces are dry, sand the edges to neaten them.

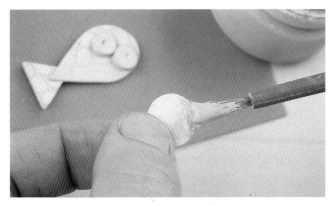

3 To join the pieces together, use a small paintbrush to apply slip to the tip of the triangle on the textured side, and attach it to the back of the pointed end of the teardrop shape to create the mermaid's tail. Then apply slip to the backs of the small circles and place them in the middle of the teardrop shape. Finally, apply slip to the back of the large circle, and place it at the top of the teardrop shape to form the mermaid's head.

4 To make the mermaid's hair, use the syringe to pipe around the edge of the circle. If you find that difficult, roll out a long, thin sausage shape from the clay and attach it with slip.

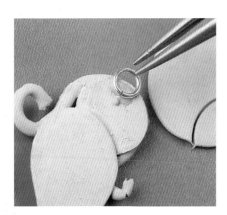

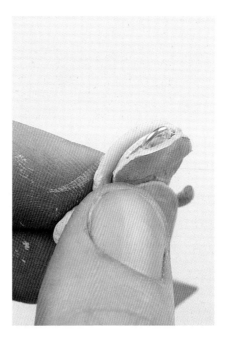

6 Place a jump ring on the top of the head, so that half of it overlaps the edge, then place the semi-circular section of clay on top so that the jump ring is sandwiched in between the two pieces of clay. Smooth over the top with the blending tool to secure it. If any pieces come away, just re-apply the slip and leave to dry again. When the mermaid is dry, it is ready to fire either in the kiln or with a butane torch on a heatproof mat or fire brick (see page 12). Once the mermaid has cooled down, polish it either in a barrel polisher or using a wire brush (see page 11).

5 Turn the mermaid over and apply a little slip to the top of the head, where the jump ring is going to be placed. Roll out some thin clay and cut out a large circle. Using a cutter, cut out a semi-circular section from the circle, as shown.

7 Thread a 2-in. (5-cm) length of 24-gauge (0.6mm) silver wire through the pearl. Using round-nose pliers, form a loop at one end of the wire and link it into the jump ring at the top of the mermaid. Then, holding the loop in flat-nose pliers, wrap any excess wire around the wire stem below the pearl (see page 20). Form another loop at the other end of the wire in the same way, thread it onto the ribbon, wrap the wire around the stem above the pearl, and trim off any excess with the wire cutters. Now open up the other jump ring, link it into the jump ring on the bell, and close the jump ring securely with the flat-nose pliers. Thread the bell onto the ribbon.

FAIRY

This design is a variation on the mermaid. You could use letter stamps to name it after your own little fairy—or even make a whole set of different characters.

W R A P O V E R
BEAD BRACELET

MATERIALS
large packet pmc3 clay
pmc3 slip
4 x silver crimp beads
7 in. (18cm) tigertail wire
1 x 12mm silver toggle clasp
8mm Indian glass beads

TOOLS
badger balm
workboard
roller and spacers
skeleton leaf
craft knife
ruler
paintbrush
sandpaper
butane torch and heatproof mat
   or fire brick, or kiln
flat-nose pliers
wire cutters

This is a great project for using up scraps of clay to make filler beads for a necklace or a bracelet. I alternated them with hand-made Indian glass beads, but you could use any beads you like. Once the pmc beads have been fired, you can polish them in a barrel polisher or with a wire brush. I used a barrel polisher to give them a shiny finish, which I think works well in combination with the hand-made glass beads.

1 Rub badger balm on your tools and hands and then, using your hands, roll the clay into a sausage shape on the workboard, turning it periodically as you would when making pastry to prevent it from sticking. The thinner you roll the clay, the more delicate the bead will be.

2 Lay the skeleton leaf on top of the clay and gently roll over the top. Peel off the leaf to reveal the textured surface.

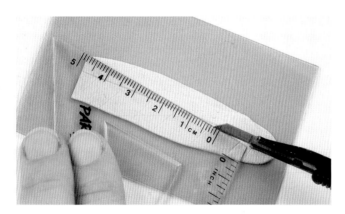

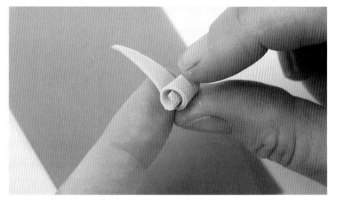

3 Using a ruler and a craft knife, cut a straight edge on one end of the clay. Now cut an elongated triangle. I made mine just over 1/2 in. (13mm) wide at the top and about 2 in. (5 cm) long.

4 Place the clay patterned side down and roll up the triangle from the wide end towards the pointed end. Paint a little slip over the end to hold it together. Make sure there is still a hole in the centre of the bead before you leave it to dry. Make at least six or seven beads. Once the beads are dry, sand and neaten the edges. The pieces are now ready to fire, either in a kiln or with a butane torch on a heatproof mat or fire brick (see page 12).

5 Slide two silver crimp beads onto the tigertail wire. Hold them near one end of the wire, thread on one half of the toggle clasp, bend the end of the wire over to form a loop, and then push the wire back down through both crimp beads. Using flat-nose pliers, press the crimp beads flat so that they grip the tigertail wire tightly. Now string on the beads, making sure you leave enough room at the other end of the bracelet for the other half of the clasp. Thread on two more crimp beads and the other half of the toggle clasp as before, using flat-nose pliers to press both crimp beads securely onto the wire. Trim off any excess wire.

VARIATION

Combine wrapover pmc beads with cut-glass beads in vibrant colours to create a pair of dangly earrings. This is a really quick and easy way of creating a matching set of jewellery to suit any occasion or outfit.

W R A P O V E R
RING

MATERIALS
large packet pmc3 clay
pmc3 slip

TOOLS
triblet
adhesive tape
strip of non-stick plastic
badger balm
workboard
roller and spacers
skeleton leaf

ruler
paintbrush
sandpaper
butane torch and heatproof
  mat or fire brick, or kiln
thin wire brush and rubber
  block, or barrel polisher

This ring is one of my favourites. I often make it with gold decoration, using the keum-boo technique described on page 114 or by soldering on gold wire shapes, but this is a plainer, simpler version. This design also avoids the problem of having a visible join on a ring.

If you wish, you can patinate the ring after firing and then repolish it to leave the leaf impression darker than the rest of the ring (see page 18).

RING SIZES CHART

US	UK	Circumference in mm	US	UK	Circumference in mm
3	F	44	8	Q	56.6
3³⁄₈	G	44.9	8⁵⁄₈	R	58.4
3³⁄₄	H	45.9	9¹⁄₈	S	59.4
4¹⁄₄	I	47.1	9⁵⁄₈	T	60.6
4⁵⁄₈	J	48.1	10¹⁄₄	U	62.2
5¹⁄₈	K	49.3	10⁵⁄₈	V	63.1
5¹⁄₂	L	50.3	11¹⁄₈	W	64.3
6	M	51.5	11⁵⁄₈	X	65.7
6¹⁄₂	N	52.8	12	Y	66.6
7	O	54	12¹⁄₂	Z	67.9
7¹⁄₂	P	55.3			

1 Measure your finger (see page 96) or have your finger or a ring measured at a jewellers. Because of the overlap and the 10 percent shrinkage of the clay during firing, you need to make the ring four sizes bigger than your actual ring size. You can work this out on a specialist ring triblet if you have access to one.

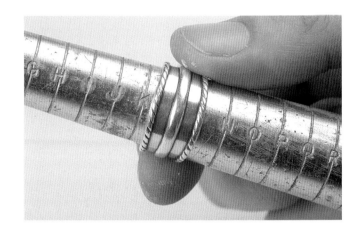

2 Make a mark on the triblet four sizes bigger than your ring size and tape a piece of non-stick plastic around the triblet at this point. (The plastic will make it easier to remove the clay when dry.) Rub badger balm on your tools and hands, then roll out the clay, using spacers to keep the thickness even. Place a skeleton leaf on top, gently roll over the top, then peel away the leaf to reveal the texture. Using a craft knife and ruler and being careful not to squash the leaf impression, cut an elongated triangle, as in Step 3 of the Wrapover Bead Bracelet on page 58. I cut a triangle just over 1/2 in. (13mm) wide x 3 in. (7.5 cm) long to allow for an overlap. Remove the excess clay and put it back in the packet to prevent it from drying out.

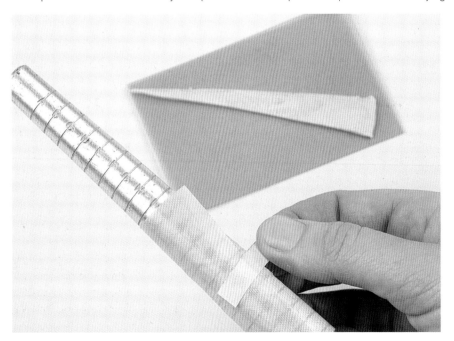

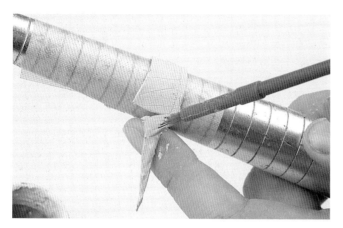

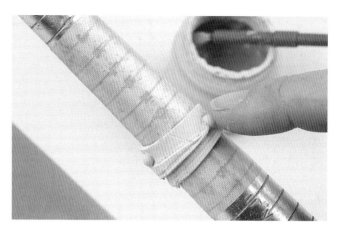

3 Pick up the clay triangle and wrap it around the triblet on top of the plastic. It is better to make the ring slightly smaller than required, as it can be stretched slightly after it has been fired by putting it on a triblet and hammering it down with a rawhide mallet. (Alternatively, get it stretched at a jewellers.) At the point where the triangle overlaps, paint some slip onto the triangular end and push it down firmly.

4 Roll three tiny balls of clay. Using slip, apply one to the very end of the triangle and the other two to what will be the front of the ring. Find somewhere to wedge the triblet securely and leave the ring to dry.

5 When the ring is dry, very carefully remove it from the triblet and sand the edges. The ring is now ready to fire, either in a kiln or with a butane torch on a heatproof mat or fire brick (see page 12). When it has cooled, polish it with a wire brush or in a barrel polisher. A barrel polisher strengthens the pmc, which is more important with rings than with other pieces of jewellery, as they get heavier wear.

MINI BOOK
PENDANT

MATERIALS

small packet pmc3 clay
5 x 5mm silver jump rings
scrap of fabric
20-in. (50-cm) length of ready-made
  chain

TOOLS

badger balm
workboard
roller and spacers
craft knife
steel ruler
texture plate
heart cutter
star cutter
bugle bead
sandpaper
round needle file
butane torch and heatproof mat
  or fire brick, or kiln
wire brush and rubber block,
  or barrel polisher
masking tape
thick needle
2 pairs flat-nose pliers

You can personalise this pendant by stamping the silver with the recipient's name or a message, using letter stamps from either jewellery or card-making suppliers. You could also embellish the fabric with your own design.
A larger version, filled with hand-made paper as a small notebook, would make a lovely christening or wedding present. Another option is to turn the pendant into a brooch by hanging it from a large safety pin.

1 Cut the clay in half. Rub badger balm on your tools and hands, then roll out one piece of clay on the workboard to a thickness of about $1/16$ in. (1 or 2mm). Place the clay on a texture plate, gently roll over it, peel it off, and lay it pattern side up on the workboard. Using a steel ruler and craft knife, mark and cut out a $1 1/4$ x 1-in. (3 x 2.5-cm) rectangle. Remove the excess clay and put it back in the packet

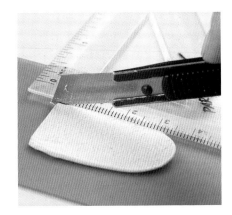

2 Using a heart cutter, cut out the heart from the centre of the top half of the rectangle. Roll out the second piece of clay, and texture it, as in Step 1. Cut out a second rectangle the same size as the first, which will become the back of the book. Instead of cutting out a heart shape, cut out a star. Put the cut-out pieces back in the packet.

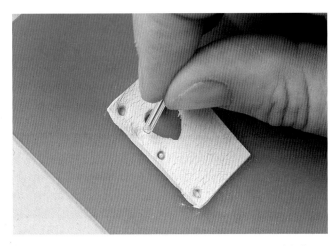

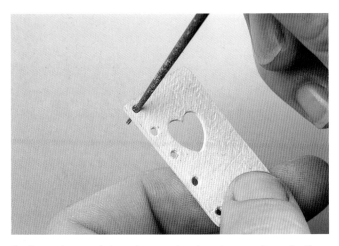

3 Using the bugle bead, punch out five evenly spaced holes on the left-hand side of the front cover and five evenly spaced holes on the right-hand side of the back cover. If you have letter stamps, you could personalise the book at this point by adding words or a name. Leave to dry.

4 Once dry, sand the edges and, using the round needle file, carefully clean up the holes. The book covers are now ready to fire, either in a kiln or with a butane torch on a heatproof mat or fire brick (see page 12). Once fired, polish the pieces with a wire brush or in a barrel polisher (see page 11).

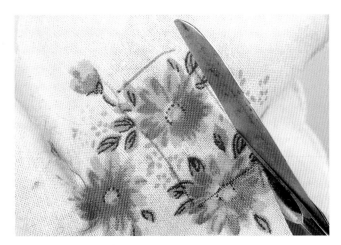

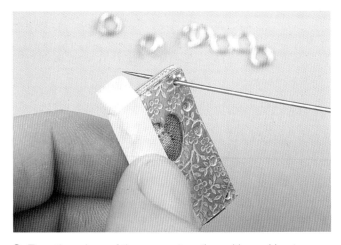

5 Cut two pieces of fabric slightly smaller than the book covers and place them inside the two covers, with the pattern side facing out. (Do not use very thick fabric.) Make sure you can see the fabric through the punched-out holes.

6 Tape the edges of the covers together with masking tape, leaving the holes visible. Using a thick needle, poke through the holes in the book cover.

7 Using flat-nose pliers, open up one of the jump rings and feed it through the top hole of the front cover. Using a second pair of flat-nose pliers, close the jump ring tightly. Repeat with the four other holes.

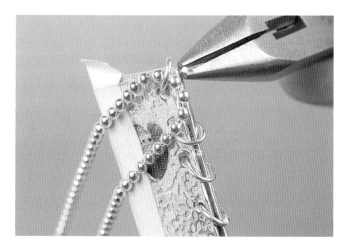

8 To complete the necklace, open up the top jump ring with flat-nose pliers and slip the chain into the ring. Close the jump ring securely and remove the masking tape.

D A I S Y
RING

MATERIALS
small packet pmc3 clay
sterling-silver band ring
syringe silver solder or silver
   solder strip

TOOLS
badger balm
workboard
roller and spacers
daisy cutter
sandpaper
paintbrush
borax
reverse-action tweezers
butane torch and heatproof mat
   or fire brick
safety pickle
plastic or brass tweezers
wire brush and rubber block,
   or barrel polisher

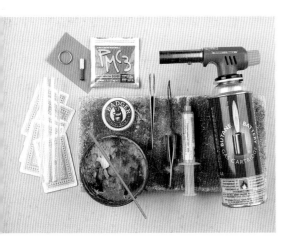

This project is a very economic way of using pmc, as it uses a store-bought sterling-silver ring as the main body and tiny pieces of pmc as delicate decorations.

In my design, the daisy motifs are wider than the ring band. If your ring band is wider than your chosen motifs, you will have to solder them slightly differently. If this is the case, apply flux and syringe solder to all three daisies, then heat each one individually until the solder flows. Drop all three into safety pickle for a few minutes, then wash. Apply flux to the backs of the daisies and the front of the ring, and solder together, following Steps 4 to 6. You may not be able to solder all three daisies in one go; if not, do one at a time, as in the step-by-step instructions.

1 Rub badger balm on your tools and hands, and roll out the clay on the workboard to a thickness of about 1/16 in. (1 or 2mm) or less. Using the cutter, cut out three daisies and leave them to dry. Once they are dry, neaten the edges with sandpaper. Fire with a butane torch (see page 12), then leave to cool.

2 Mix some borax flux (see page 13). Using a paintbrush, apply a little to the back of each daisy and also to the front of the ring at the points where you are going to attach the daisies. Put the daisies on the heatproof mat or fire brick. Pick up the ring with reverse-action tweezers, and place it on the back of one of the daisies.

3 Still holding the ring in the tweezers, squeeze a little dab of syringe solder next to where the daisy and the ring join. If using solder strip, cut a small piece, dip it in the flux, and use tweezers to place it next to where the daisy and the ring join.

4 Light the butane torch and heat the ring (see page 13). You need to heat the whole ring, not just the daisy. Once the silver reaches the temperature at which the solder melts, the solder will flow along the join.

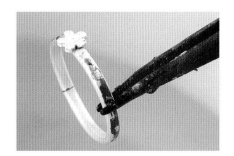

5 Turn off the torch and drop the ring into the safety pickle (see page 14).

6 Leave the ring in the pickle for a few minutes, then remove it using plastic or brass tweezers and wash it in water. Repeat Steps 4 and 5 to solder the other two daisies in place, making sure that you space them evenly. Do not overheat the ring, otherwise the solder on the other daisies may remelt and cause them to slip out of position. Polish the ring in a barrel polisher or with a wire brush.

CHAPTER 2

SILICONE MOLDS

P I G
CUFFLINKS

MATERIALS
small packet pmc3 clay
1 pack two-part silicone rubber
2 x ready-made silver cufflink chains
4 x 6mm large silver jump rings

TOOLS
pig-shaped button
badger balm
flat-nose pliers
tweezers
rubber blending tool
sandpaper
needle file
craft knife
kiln
safety pickle
wire brush and rubber block,
   or barrel polisher

These little cufflinks make a great gift! I have chosen pigs, but you can choose a different motif that is more personal to the wearer. You can use a ready-made mold or make your own, as I did, from shaped buttons— a great source of interesting shapes for mold making.

1 Choose an object to use as a mold. Following the manufacturer's instructions, mix together enough of the two-part silicone mix to surround the button.

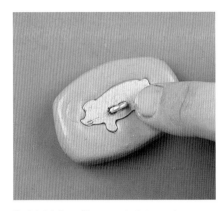

2 Mold the silicone mix into a shape similar to that of the button, and flatten the top of the silicone. Push the button into the silicone mix until the flat back is level with the top of the silicone. Leave the silicone to harden, which takes around 15 minutes. Flex the mold to release the button, which will come out cleanly.

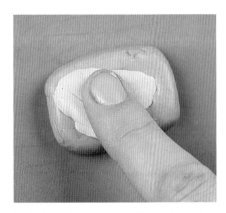

3 Rub badger balm on the mold and on your hands to prevent the clay from sticking. Push a piece of clay into the mold until the mold is filled and the clay is flat and level with the top.

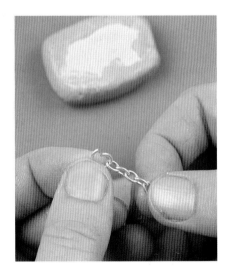

4 Using your flat-nose pliers, open a jump ring, thread on the end link of a cufflink chain, and close the jump ring again.

5 Holding the jump ring with tweezers, push it into the clay, join side down, until only half of it protrudes above the surface. Do not push it too far down in the mold.

6 Using a rubber blending tool, smooth some clay over the middle of the jump ring to secure it in place. Leave the piece to dry.

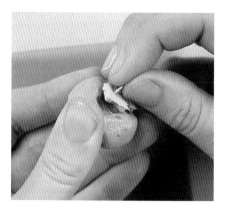

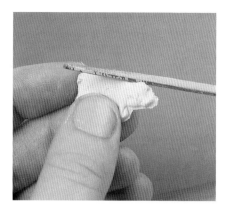

7 Turn the mold upside down and flex the silicone slightly to release the pig. Repeat Steps 3 to 6 to make the second cufflink.

8 File and sand the edges of the cufflinks to neaten them and define the shape clearly.

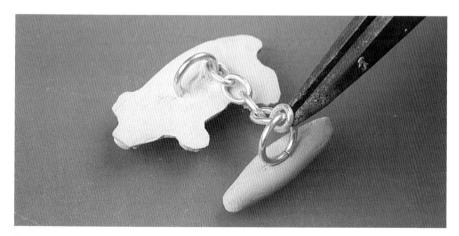

9 Now make the bars for the other end of the cufflink chains. Roll a small piece of clay into a sausage shape about 3/4 in. (2 cm) long, cut it to length, and taper both ends. Using your flat-nose pliers, open a jump ring, link it into the other end of the cufflink chain that is attached to the pig, and close it up. Holding the jump ring in a pair of tweezers, push it halfway into the sausage shape and smooth clay over the jump ring, as in Step 6. Leave to dry.

10 Sand both ends of the bars, then fire the cufflinks in the kiln on a pmc3 fast setting. (They can be fired with a torch, but you must be very careful not to melt the chains.) After firing, place the cufflinks in safety pickle (see page 14) to remove any black oxide, then polish in a barrel polisher or with a wire brush (see page 11).

D E T A C H A B L E
CHARM BRACELET

MATERIALS
1 pack of two-part silicone rubber
large packet pmc3 clay
2 x 8mm silver jump rings per charm
1 silver trigger clasp per charm
coloured feature bead
1 silver headpin per bead
ready-made silver chain bracelet

TOOLS
selection of objects to make molds
  (or ready-made silicone molds)
badger balm
tweezers
rubber blending tool
sandpaper
flat file
butane torch and heatproof mat
  or fire brick, or kiln
safety pickle
wire brush and rubber block,
  or barrel polisher
flat-nose pliers
round-nose pliers
wire cutters

This versatile and very personal piece of jewellery uses a ready-made chain bracelet—although if you're an experienced jeweller you could, of course, make your own. Each charm can be detached from the chain, so you can change the design to suit your mood or the occasion. You can also colour coordinate the bracelet to suit a particular outfit, by incorporating a feature bead, as I have done.

You can use found objects to make your own silicone molds, and reuse the molds to make matching pieces of jewellery. If you don't want to make your mold, there are many ready-made ones on the market.

1 Find objects that you would like on your bracelet, and make a mold for each one (see pages 11 and 72). Rub badger balm on the molds and on your hands to prevent the clay from sticking. Push a piece of clay into each mold until the mold is filled and the clay is level with the top.

2 Using a pair of tweezers, push a jump ring into the clay, join side down, until only half of it protrudes above the surface, positioning it near the top of the mold and at a slight angle from the vertical. Using a rubber blending tool, smooth the clay on the back of the charm. Leave to dry, then remove the charms from the molds by flexing the silicone (see page 73). Sand and neaten the edges. Fire the charms, either in a kiln on a pmc fast firing or with a butane torch on a heatproof mat or fire brick. Place the charms in safety pickle (see page 14) to remove any black oxide. Polish in a barrel polisher or with a wire brush.

3 Using flat-nose pliers, open a jump ring, link it through both the jump ring on the charm and a trigger clasp, and close the jump ring securely.

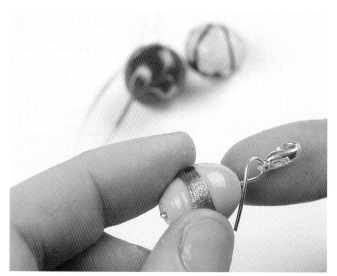

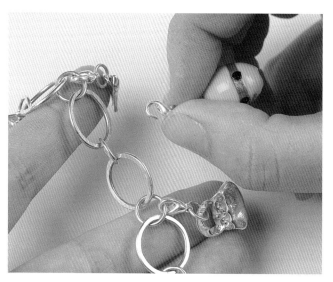

4 Thread your chosen bead and a trigger clasp onto a silver headpin and, using round-nose pliers, bend the wire of the headpin into a loop. Wrap any excess wire around the stem of the headpin below the clasp. Trim off any excess wire with wire cutters and file the end.

5 Attach the coloured bead to the charm bracelet via the trigger clasp. You can change the bead to match the colour of your outfit.

S T A R F I S H
EARRINGS

MATERIALS
16g pmc3 clay
2 x 8mm cubic zirconias
2 x silver earring posts and butterfly
  studs
pmc syringe

TOOLS
badger balm
starfish mold
rubber blending tool
pin or piece of wire
tweezers
sandpaper
kiln
wire brush and rubber block, or barrel
  polisher

A ready-made mold was ued to make these starfish earrings, but you could make your own using a favorite shell. The starfish motif would also look great as a pendant; you could combine it with shell beads to create a sea-themed necklace. I chose a triangular stone for the centres, but a different shape would work just as well.

It is possible to buy earring posts that are specially made with a layer of fine silver on them so that they will not oxidize (blacken) during firing. If you can't get hold of these, use sterling silver posts with a base and clean them after firing. Alternatively, if you are able to do silver soldering, wait until the starfish have been fired and then solder the backs in place (see page 13).

1 Rub badger balm on the mold and on your hands to prevent the clay from sticking. Form a piece of clay into a rough starfish shape and start pushing it into the mold.

2 Using a rubber blending tool, push the clay into the corners of the mold. You can always remove a little clay if you put in too much.

3 Before the clay dries, bend back the mold and remove the starfish shape. Repeat Steps 1 to 3 to make the second earring motif.

4 Using a pin, make a small hole in the centre of each starfish. (This is where the stones will be placed; the holes allow the air to escape from under the stones during firing.)

5 Using tweezers, push one cubic zirconia stone into the middle of each starfish, being careful not to damage the detail.

6 Once the stone is level, use the blending tool to push clay over the edge of the stone. (Make sure it is well covered, as the clay will shrink when fired. If your stone is deep, you will have to build up a lip of clay around it.) Neaten the edges of the settings using the blending tool.

7 Carefully turn the starfish over. Lightly roughen the back of the starfish with the blending tool. Place each earring post in position, slightly above centre. Cover with extra clay or squeeze a blob of pmc syringe on to the back of the starfish and press the earring post into position, then apply a little syringe paste over the back of the post. Leave to dry in a warm place; because the starfish are quite thick, they will take longer to dry.

8 Carefully sand any rough areas, leaving the front of the starfish untouched. Now it is ready to fire in the kiln on a pmc fast setting (see page 12). (You could fire both starfish with a butane torch, but it is easy to overheat the earring posts and melt them.) These earrings look best really shiny, so if possible polish them in a barrel polisher. Push the studs onto the backs.

VARIATION

To make a matching necklace, push a jump ring into the back of the starfish to create a pendant bail for the chain or cord.

C U P C A K E
POT

MATERIALS
1 pack two-part silicone
   rubber
2 large packets pmc3 clay

pmc3 slip
1 x 8mm red glass bead

TOOLS
paper petit-four cases
badger balm
roller and spacers
workboard
craft knife
texture plate
1½-in. (4-cm) circle
   cutter
doming block
pin or thin wire
sandpaper
round needle file
rubberblending tool

¼-in. (6mm) daisy cutter
¼-in. (6mm) heart cutter
paintbrush
kiln
wire brush and rubber
   block, or barrel polisher
wire cutters
round-nose pliers
flat-nose pliers

Use this colourful little cupcake pot to store rings in.
Alternatively, just make it as an ornament. To give it
more colour, you could add some enamel to the top of
the cupcake (see page 15) or use a different bead or
object on the top. It would be fun to make different
sweets to go with it.

   I used a doming block to make the "lid" of the
cupcake, but if you don't have one you can mold the
clay to the right shape by placing it on a light bulb or
similar dome-shaped object and leaving it to dry.
Alternatively, make a dome from silicone rubber, using
the petit-four case as a guide.

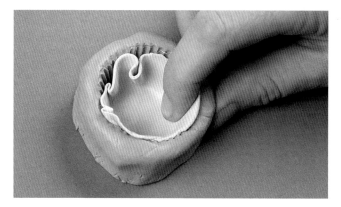

1 Following the manufacturer's instructions, mix enough of the two-part silicone mix to enclose a petit-four case. Take a stack of the cases and push them straight down into the silicone. (A single case is not strong enough to push into the rubber.) Do not push the cases right down to the bottom of the rubber, as this would make the base of the mold thin and weak. Leave the silicone to harden, then remove the cases.

2 Rub badger balm on your tools and hands to prevent the clay from sticking, then roll out the clay on a workboard, using spacers to keep the thickness even. Gently ease the clay into the mold, in the same way as you would when making a pastry case; it is very important to push it into the fluted detailling around the sides of the mold.

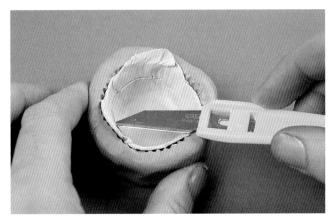

3 Take a craft knife and trim off the top of the clay. (I cut about two-thirds of the way down the mold to reduce the size.) Don't worry if the edge is not completely straight, as you can file it straight later. Leave the clay to dry.

4 Gently flex the silicone and carefully lever the dry clay out of the mold.

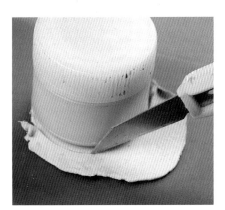

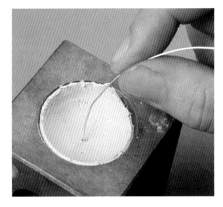

5 Roll out more clay for the lid of the pot, placing three playing cards on either side of your workboard as spacers. Lay the clay on top of the texture plate, and gently roll over the back of the clay. Cut out a circle that is slightly smaller in diameter than the base of the cupcake.

6 Lay the clay pattern side down in a suitable doming block indent, making sure you push it right down to the bottom. (Don't push too hard as you will damage the pattern.) Using a piece of wire, make a small hole in the middle of the circle and leave the clay to dry.

7 Remove the lid from the mold (you may find that it is a slightly different shape from the base). Place each piece upside down on a flat surface on a medium grade of piece of sandpaper, and carefully sand them until the edges are completely level.

9 Using a paintbrush, apply slip to the backs of the heart and the daisy. Place the heart in the bottom of the cupcake base and the daisy inside the lid. Make sure that the small hole in the top of the daisy is still there. Sand out any imperfections and fill any cracks with slip. Fire in the kiln on a pmc fast setting (see page 12). Polish in a barrel polisher or with a wire brush (see page 11).

8 Roll out a little more clay quite thinly. Using the cutters, cut one daisy and one heart. Using a piece of wire, make a small hole in the middle of the daisy.

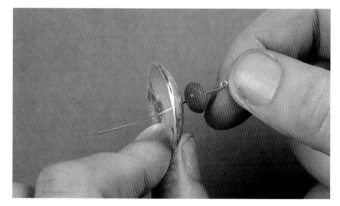

10 Cut a short length of thin silver wire and, using round-nose pliers, form the end into a very small loop. Slide the red bead onto the wire, then push the wire through the hole in the top of the cupcake. Trim the wire to around ³⁄₈ in. (1 cm). Using round-nose pliers, form another loop at the other end of the wire, then hold the loop in your flat-nose pliers and coil the wire around to form a spiral that sits tight against the base of the bead (see page 19).

VARIATION

Instead of putting a red bead on top, I used a coloured brad, of the kind used in card making, which makes an effective "handle."

CHAPTER 3

HOLLOW FORMS

RIBBONED
HEART BEAD

MATERIALS
small piece cork clay
syringe pmc3
2 x 16-in. (40-cm) lengths of 1/4-in.
  (6-mm) ribbon
2 x 9mm silver square calottes
1x 5mm trigger clasp

TOOLS
skewer
sandpaper
butane torch and heatproof mat
  or fire brick, or kiln
wire brush and rubber block,
  or barrel polisher
needle file
flat-nose pliers

These fantastic feature beads, in which coloured ribbon can be glimpsed through gaps in the clay, take a little practice to create, but are well worth the effort. Start by piping cake icing: it's a much less expensive option until you've mastered the technique!

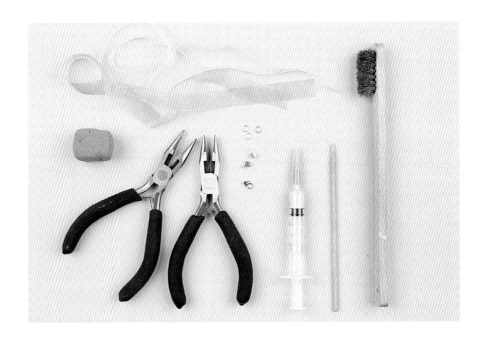

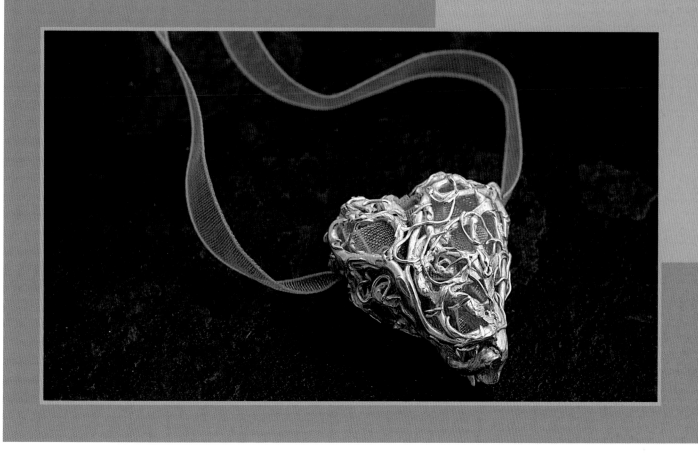

1 Shape a piece of cork clay into a basic heart shape about 1¼ in. (3 cm) high; the cork clay will burn away in firing and the bead will shrink by around 10 percent.

2 Push a skewer all the way through the clay and reshape the heart. Leave it to dry for a whole day. You must make sure that the cork clay is completely dry before firing.

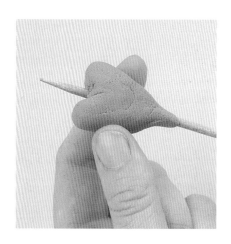

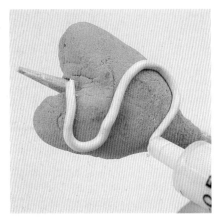

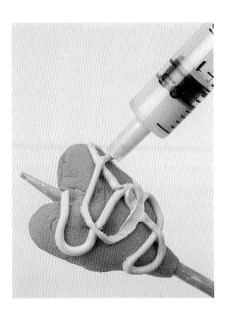

3 First, use the syringe pmc without the nozzle to create a thick line. Place the end of the tube on the cork clay and slowly and gently push down on the end of the plunger.

4 Pipe the syringe clay over the surface in a random pattern, turning the heart as you go so that you don't leave any large gaps. You don't have to make a continuous line: you can stop piping and restart somewhere else if you wish. Try not to touch the syringed clay, as it tends to pull away from the cork clay.

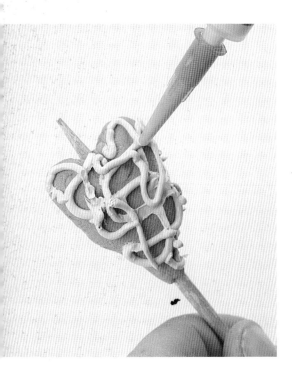

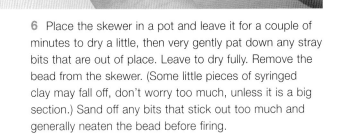

5 Put a small nozzle on the syringe clay and go over the surface again to create thinner lines. Make sure that there are no loose ends.

6 Place the skewer in a pot and leave it for a couple of minutes to dry a little, then very gently pat down any stray bits that are out of place. Leave to dry fully. Remove the bead from the skewer. (Some little pieces of syringed clay may fall off, don't worry too much, unless it is a big section.) Sand off any bits that stick out too much and generally neaten the bead before firing.

7 Fire the bead—ideally in a kiln, although you can use a butane torch (see page 12). Most of the cork clay in the middle will burn away during firing, but there may be some residue left. Poke a pin or needle file through the holes to break up the remaining cork clay, then shake it out of the bead. (This can be quite a messy procedure.)

8 Polish the bead with a wire brush; you can't polish the interior of the bead, but as you are putting ribbon inside you won't see the interior anyway. Alternatively, use a barrel polisher; the steel shot inside the barrel polisher may get stuck inside the bead, but you can shake it out.

9 Take one length of ribbon and feed it into an opening in the bead, pushing it into the middle with the end of a needle file. To finish, thread a second length of ribbon around one of the wires of the bead and tie a knot, leaving the same amount of ribbon extending on each side. Place each end of the ribbon in a square callotte and hold it there with flat-nose pliers. Use a second pair of pliers to close the flaps over the end of the ribbon to secure it. Fit a trigger clasp to one callotte.

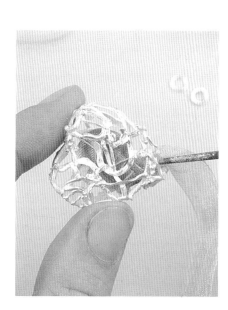

VARIATION

Here, I simply changed the shape of the cork clay base from a heart to a cube; I then added a faceted stone to one bead and hung a small bell from the other.

S T A R
NECKLACE

MATERIALS

cork clay
small packet pmc3 clay
pmc3 slip
1¼ x 1½-in. (3 x 4-cm)
   piece of paper pmc
liver of sulphur or Platinol
18 in. (45 cm) tigertail wire
20 x 6mm sodalite star
   beads

6 x 18mm Biwa pearls
4 x 6mm fluorite beads
2 x 18mm shell beads
16 x 1mm silver crimp
   beads
1 x 12mm silver toggle
   clasp

TOOLS

skewer
badger balm
roller and spacers
workboard
texture plate
1¼-in. (3-cm) circle cutter
craft knife
paintbrush
rubber blending tool
flat needle file
sandpaper
½-in. (13mm) star cutter
½-in. (13mm) circle cutter
bugle bead to make holes
kiln
wire brush and rubber
   block, or barrel polisher
wire cutters
flat-nose pliers

Combined with pearls and star-shaped beads, this striking feature bead makes a wonderful centrepiece for a necklace. I used sodalite to represent the night sky. You could also change the shape of the bead and the motifs applied to it to flowers, circles, or hearts.

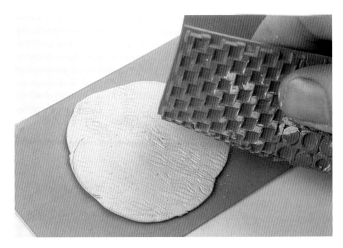

1 Using your fingers, mold a piece of cork clay into the shape you want the bead to be; I made a flattened circle about 1¼ in. (3 cm) in diameter. Push a skewer through the cork clay, making sure it is just above the centre, and reshape the cork clay. Leave the clay to dry overnight or longer; it must be completely dry before firing.

2 Rub badger balm on your hand and tools, and roll out three-quarters of the pmc3 clay on a workboard to a thickness of about ¹⁄₁₆ in. (1 or 2mm). Gently dab the texture plate over the clay.

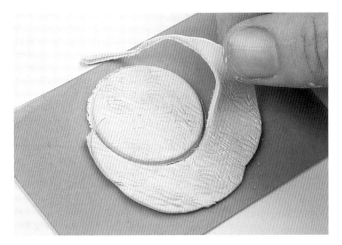

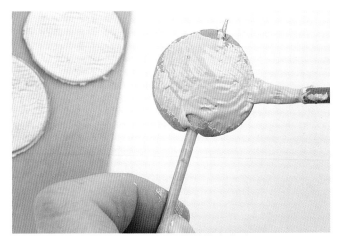

3 Using a large circle cutter, cut out two circles of clay; alternatively, cut around a can or glass of the appropriate size, using a craft knife. Remove the excess clay and put it back in the packet.

4 Using a paintbrush, paint slip over the cork clay to help the pmc clay adhere.

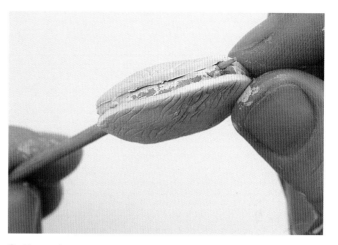

5 Place one pmc circle on the front of the cork clay and one on the back, textured side out.

6 Press the edges of the circles together to join the two circles all the way around.

7 Paint slip over the join and smooth it over with the rubber blending tool. Make sure that the seam is well joined all the way around, as it can split open during firing. Leave the bead to dry. Once it is dry, neaten the seam with a needle file and sandpaper.

8 Take out the paper pmc, which feels very different to pmc clay; it also doesn't dry out. Using the star cutter, cut out as many stars as you can fit onto both sides of the bead. If you don't have any paper pmc, use leftover clay and roll it out very thinly.

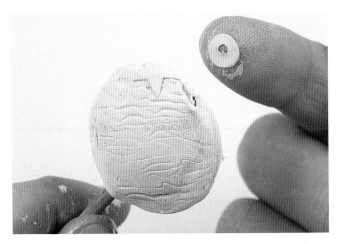

9 Paint slip over the back of the stars, and place them on the bead. Place some slip across the join, as this will strengthen it. Make sure that the stars are well stuck down, then leave them to dry.

10 To neaten the holes top and bottom, cut out two small circles of clay and make a small hole in the middle of each one with the end of a bugle bead. Paint slip on the back and place the circles over the holes, then leave the bead to dry. Carefully pull out the skewer and sand the edges of the holes. Fire the bead in the kiln on a pmc3 fast setting. Leave the bead to cool, then polish it in a barrel polisher or with a wire brush (see page 11). (If you are using a barrel polisher, make sure you have got the residue from the cork clay out of the centre of the bead, otherwise the cork clay will make a mess inside the barrel polisher. You can clean the bead by washing it under running water.)

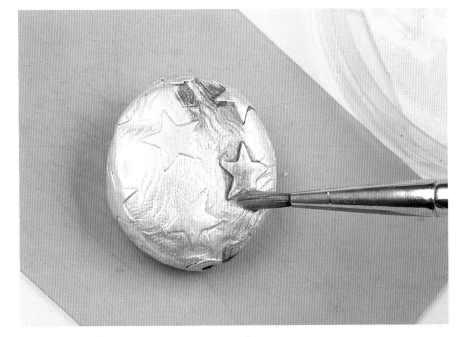

11 If you want to give the bead an antique look, patinate it (see page 18). Mix up a weak solution of liver of sulphur in a glass jar, following the instructions carefully. Place the bead on a piece of wire, hold it under hot running water, then dip it in the solution until you get the colour that you want. Alternatively, use Platinol.

12 Centre the feature bead on the tigertail wire, then thread your chosen beads on either side to form the centre of the necklace. (Refer to the photograph on page 90.)

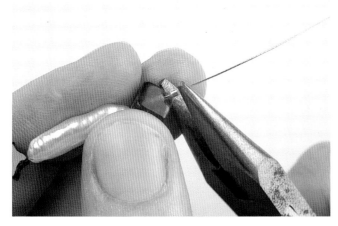

13 When you have put on all the central beads, thread a crimp bead onto each side and crimp in place (see page 22). About ½ in. (1 cm) further along the wire, add another crimp bead and then a star. Repeat, spacing stars evenly, until you get to about 1½ in. (4 cm) from the end of the wire. Slip two silver crimp beads and the toggle clasp onto one end, bend the wire back down through the crimp beads, and crimp the beads in place.

VARIATION

Painting the beads with stripes of Platinol creates a striking design that is complemented by the brightly coloured turquoise chips.

C U B I C
ZIRCONIA RING

MATERIALS
pmc3 syringe
6 x 3mm cubic zirconias

TOOLS
strip of paper
scissors
black marker pen
ruler
non-stick plastic
adhesive tape
triblet
pin
tweezers
rubber blending tool
paintbrush
sandpaper
kiln
barrel polisher

This ring is made using syringe pmc, and features an organic, free-flowing design that is reminiscent of Celtic knotwork. The tiny cubic zirconias add a little sparkle.

The sizing of rings in pmc is more difficult than in traditional jewellery because of the shrinkage. Pmc3 shrinks by about 10 percent during firing, which means that you need to make the ring four sizes larger than your actual size. If you are using a different type of clay, check the chart on page 60 to see how much shrinkage you need to allow for. If your ring is a little too small after firing, you can stretch it slightly by tapping it gently down the triblet with a leather mallet—but be very careful not to split it.

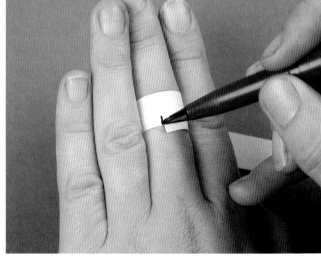

1 Measure your finger or have your finger or a ring measured at a jewellers. Alternatively, cut a strip of paper, wrap it around the widest part of your finger, and make a mark where the paper overlaps.

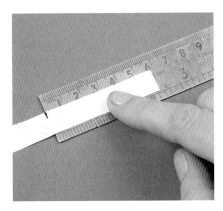 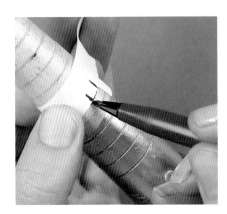 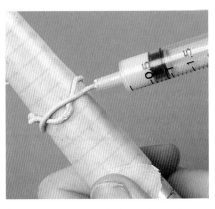

2 If you don't have a triblet, measure the length of the marked piece of paper on a ruler and check it against the chart on page 60 to get your finger size. To ensure that the ring will be the right size after the clay has shrunk during the firing process, add four sizes.

3 Cut a piece of paper to the required length. Tape a strip of non-stick plastic around the triblet, with the paper on top. Using a marker pen, mark on the paper the point at which you want the ring to start.

4 Take off the nozzle from the syringe pmc. Holding the triblet in one hand and the syringe in the other, push down on the plunger to get an even flow of syringe pmc, slowly turning the triblet as you go.

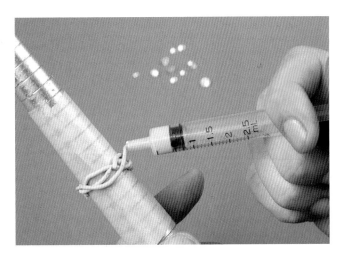 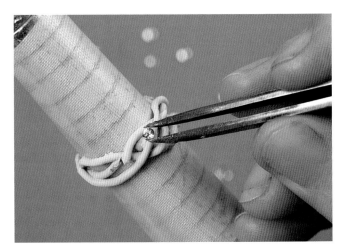

5 Go around the triblet about three times. If there are areas where the clay does not stick properly, remove the clay and lay more syringe pmc over the top. This technique takes a little practice, and it is best to touch the clay as little as possible.

6 When you are happy with the result, take a pin and poke small holes through the clay at the points where you are going to put the cubic zirconias. This is to allow the air to escape from behind the stones during firing. Using tweezers, carefully place a cubic zirconia over each hole.

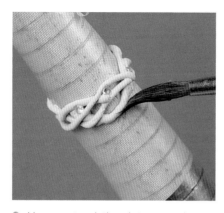

7 Using the rubber blending tool, push the stones into the clay, so that the widest parts are well below the surface. The clay will shrink, so the stones will fall out if they are not set in well. Try not to touch the clay. Find somewhere safe to wedge the triblet.

8 Use a wet paintbrush to smooth any areas that you are not happy with, then leave the ring to dry.

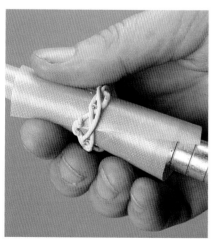

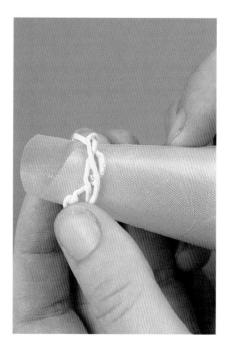

9 When it is dry, carefully remove the ring (still on the non-stick plastic) from the triblet.

10 Gently remove the ring from the non-stick plastic. It is quite easy to break the ring at this stage. Gently sand the edge and make sure there is no clay on the surface of the stones. Fire the ring in a kiln on a pmc3 fast setting, because cubic zirconias withstand high temperatures. (You could torch fire it, but it is much harder to maintain an even temperature with a ring.) Polish the ring—preferably in a barrel polisher, as this strengthens the pmc. This is important because rings get heavy wear.

CHAPTER 4

PMC AND OTHER MATERIALS

WILLOW PATTERN
PENDANT

MATERIALS
small packet pmc3 clay
pmc3 syringe
pmc3 slip
ceramic fragment
16-in. (40-cm) thin ribbon
2 x silver callottes
1 x 5mm silver bolt ring

TOOLS
badger balm
workboard
roller and spacers
craft knife
paintbrush
rubber blending tool
texture plate
silicone butterfly mold
sandpaper
kiln
wire brush and rubber block,
  or barrel polisher
2 pairs flat-nose pliers

If you've broken a favourite plate and can't bear to part with it, this is the perfect way to preserve it. I used a fragment from a traditional willow-pattern plate, but there are endless possibilities. You could also make a bracelet out of lots of pieces linked together.

This project is only suitable if you have the use of a kiln. The piece must be fired on a pmc slow setting, so that it heats up slowly and is fired at a lower temperature for a longer time than normal. If fired at too high a heat, the ceramic fragment may crack. When firing is complete, let the piece cool down naturally; do not open the door of the kiln straight away, as the sudden change in temperature could cause the ceramic fragment to crack.

1 Rub badger balm on your hands and tools, and roll some of the clay into a long sausage shape. When it is long enough to go all the way around the ceramic fragment, roll over it with the roller to create a long ribbon, making sure that it is wider than the edge of the ceramic piece. Cut off one end, so that it is straight.

2 Paint slip along the edges of the ceramic fragment.

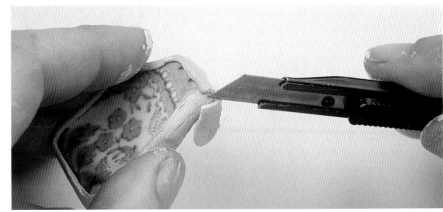

3 Starting at the top, position the ribbon of clay around the edges of the ceramic fragment to form a bezel, or setting, making sure that the clay overhangs both the back and the front of the ceramic piece.

4 Trim off the overlap, secure the join with a little more slip, and smooth over the join with the rubber blending tool.

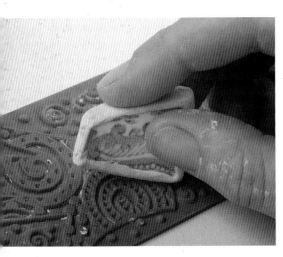

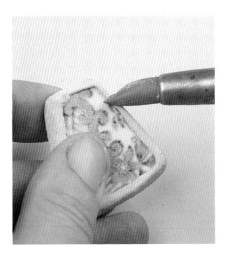

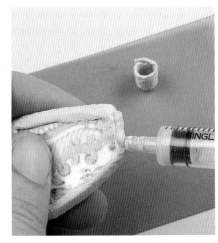

5 Roll the edges of the clay bezel on a texture plate to impress the pattern into it.

6 Using your fingers and the rubber blending tool, push the edges of the clay bezel over the sides of the ceramic piece, being careful not to push too hard and split the clay. Neaten the clay as much as possible, using the rubber blending tool. If there are any cracks, paint a little slip in them.

7 Roll out more clay, place it on the texture plate, and roll over it again. Using a craft knife, cut a 1¼ x ³⁄₈-in. (3 x 1-cm) rectangle and roll it up into a tube shape to form the bail through which you can loop the hanging ribbon in Step 11. Paint slip along the join. Syringe some pmc along the top of the pendant, so that you can attach the bail.

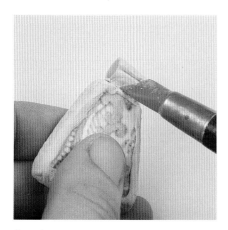

8 Paint slip along the top edge of the pendant and press the bail into place. If the join is weak, paint on a little more slip. Neaten the join with the rubber blending tool.

9 Make a butterfly from pmc, using a ready-made silicone mold (see page 11).

10 Attach the butterfly to the top of the pendant with slip and leave to dry.

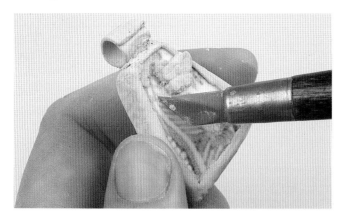

11 When the pendant is dry, sand any rough edges and, most importantly, remove any excess clay from the surface of the ceramic using the rubber blending tool. Fire in a kiln on a pmc slow setting, then leave to cool. Polish in a barrel polisher or with a wire brush. Feed the ribbon through the bail. Place each end of the ribbon in a square callotte and hold it in place with a pair of flat-nose pliers. Using a second pair of flat-nose pliers, close the flaps over the end of the ribbon to secure it. Fit a silver bolt ring on one side.

VARIATIONS

The pieces of ceramic used in two of these pendants were either found, or dug up in the garden—a great way to preserve history!

DICHROIC
TRIANGLE PENDANT

MATERIALS
large packet pmc3 clay
pmc3 slip
3/4-in. (2-cm) square of pmc paper
1 x 6mm silver jump ring
1 x 10mm dichroic triangle
8 x 13mm triangular pearls
2 x 10mm star pearls
8 x 18mm pearls
approx. 50 seed beads
6 x 1mm crimp beads
18 in. (45 cm) tigertail wire

TOOLS
badger balm
work board
roller and spacers
texture plate
paintbrush
craft knife
1-in. (2.5-cm) triangle cutter
1/2-in. (13mm) triangle cutter
tweezers
rubber blending tool
needle file
sandpaper
kiln
wire brush and rubber block,
  or barrel polisher
wire cutters
flat-nose pliers

Dichroic glass is a special glass that will withstand high temperatures. It has an iridescent, metallic look, often in vibrant colours, and makes a stunning centerpiece for a pendant, as each piece of glass is unique.

This pendant uses a triangular piece of glass as the main feature; the colour reminds me of opals. The aim is not to create a perfectly geometric design, but something that looks truly hand made. Here, I've added a hand-made pmc clasp in the same shape as the pendant for a really unique finishing touch.

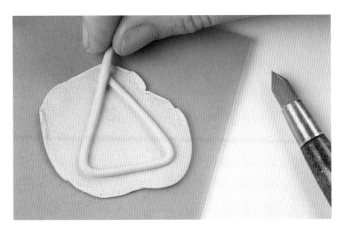

1 Apply badger balm to your hands and tools to prevent the clay from sticking, and roll out two-thirds of the clay quite thickly, at least three cards thick. Place the clay on the texture plate, roll over it again, and peel off the clay to reveal an impression of the texture. Put the clay to one side.

2 From the remainder of the clay, roll out a long, thin sausage shape about 4 in. (10 cm) long, trying to keep it an even thickness. Place the sausage shape on top of the rolled-out clay and arrange it in a rough triangle shape. This will create the border around the triangular piece of glass. The corners will be slightly rounded.

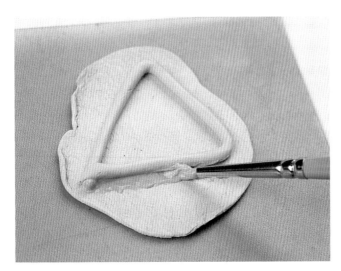

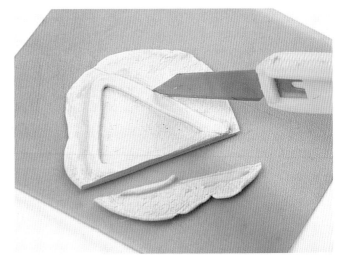

3 Paint slip around the outside edge of the clay triangle to join the two pieces together. Gently roll over the top of the border with the roller to flatten it slightly. (Do not to press hard, or you will distort the shape.)

4 Using a craft knife, cut around the edge of the outside of the triangle. (You can use a ruler to help you or do it freehand.) Remove the excess clay and replace it in the packet.

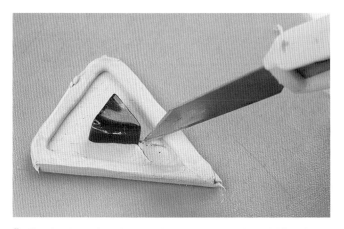

5 Gently place the piece of dichroic glass in the middle of the triangle. Using the tip of the craft knife, mark out a small diamond shape above the glass, then remove the glass and carefully cut out the diamond shape. Don't worry if the edges of the diamond are a little untidy, as you can neaten them later, when the clay is dry.

6 Now make the clasp. Roll out more clay and texture it with the mat that you used in Step 1. Using the large triangle cutter, cut out a triangle, remove the excess clay and put it to one side. Then cut a small triangle from the middle of the large triangle. Leave the large triangle to dry.

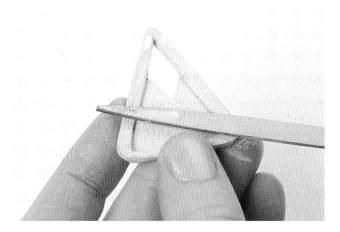

7 Using the excess clay from Step 6, roll out a small sausage shape wider than the triangular clasp. Using tweezers, pick up a silver jump ring and push it into the middle of the sausage shape, join side down, until only half of it protrudes above the surface. Using a rubber blending tool, smooth some clay over the middle of the jump ring to secure it in place. Leave to dry.

8 When the main triangle is dry, file the edges straight. If the join is visible between the base and the edge, add a little slip to the edges to hide it. File across the front of the piece to flatten the border, then sand the edges to remove the file marks.

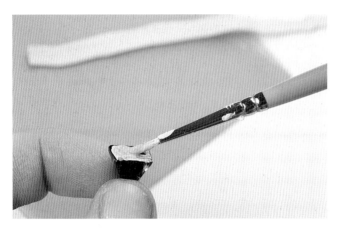

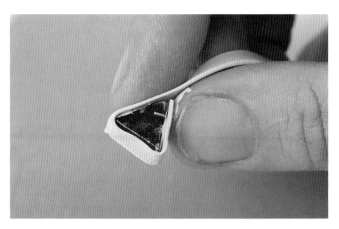

9 To set the piece of dichroic glass, roll out a sausage shape of clay. When it is long enough to go around the piece of glass, roll over it with the roller to create a long ribbon, making sure that it is wider than the circumference of the glass. Cut off one end of the clay ribbon, so that it is straight. Paint slip onto the edge of the glass.

10 Lay the ribbon of clay on the glass, starting at a corner, as it is easier to hide the join here. Wrap the clay around the circumference of the glass, trim off the overlap, secure the join with a little more slip, and smooth over the clay with the rubber blending tool. You can trim the width down if required.

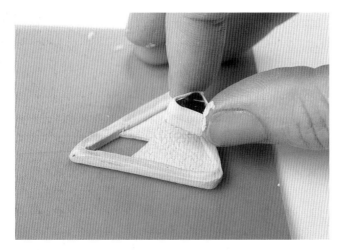

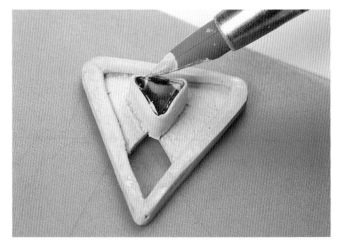

11 Paint slip thickly on the bottom of both the glass and the setting. Place the glass in the middle of the triangle, so that one corner of the glass is positioned at the base of the cut-out diamond. Carefully smooth around the base of the setting.

12 Smooth the clay slightly over the edge of the glass, making sure there is no residue of clay left on the front of the glass. Leave it to dry.

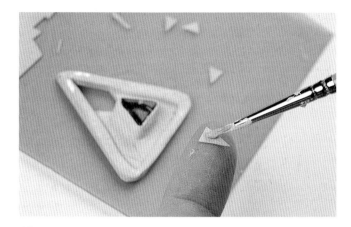

13 Cut some small triangles from paper clay, making sure they are small enough to fit inside the space between the glass and the edge of the pendant. Paint the backs of the triangles with slip, place them on to the pendant, and leave to dry. Sand and neaten all areas. Fire in the kiln on a pmc3 slow setting, which allows the glass to heat up slowly (see page 12). Allow the piece to cool down naturally in the kiln, then polish it with a wire brush or in a barrel polisher (see page 11).

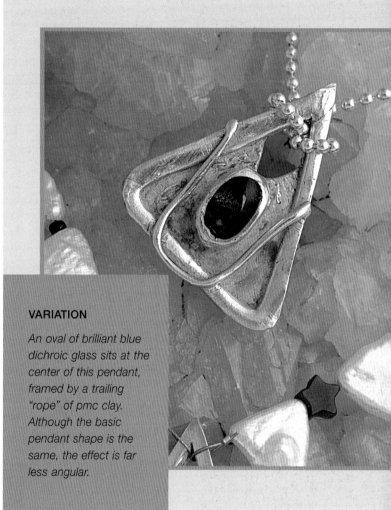

VARIATION

An oval of brilliant blue dichroic glass sits at the center of this pendant, framed by a trailing "rope" of pmc clay. Although the basic pendant shape is the same, the effect is far less angular.

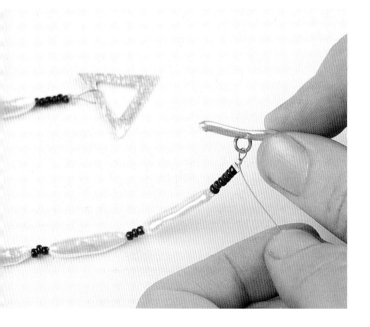

14 Cut the tigertail wire in half. Slide a crimp bead onto one piece, wrap the wire around one side of the diamond-shaped hole, push the end back through the crimp bead, and squeeze the crimp bead with flat-nose pliers. Thread on your chosen beads. When you are about 1 in. (2–3 cm) from the end, attach another crimp bead to hold the other beads in place. Repeat on the other side. Finally, attach the two parts of the toggle clasp you have made, by crimping the ends of the wire to them (see page 22).

E N A M E L
EARRINGS

MATERIALS

small packet pmc3 clay
3 enamels in different
  colours
2 x 5mm glass beads

2 1/2 in. (6 cm) 24-gauge
  (0.6mm) silver wire
2 silver ear wires

TOOLS

badger balm
workboard
roller and spacers
screw head
screwdriver bit
thin silver wire
straight cutting edge or
  craft knife and ruler

sandpaper
round needle file
fine paintbrush
kiln
barrel polisher
wire cutters
round-nose pliers
flat-nose pliers

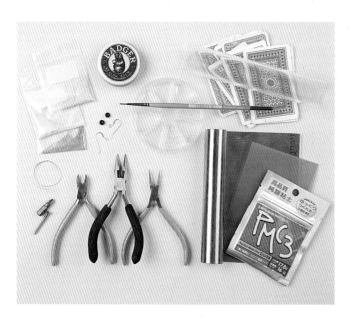

Precious metal clay is perfect for enamelling onto, as there is no need to clean it after it has been fired. These earrings demonstrate champlevé enamelling, which means filling a recessed cell with enamel—a fantastic way of adding colour to a piece of silver. The recesses are created by pressing a small object into the surface of the clay. I used the head of an ordinary household screw, but feel free to experiment with other objects to see what pattern they make. The edge of a small coin, the blunt end of a pencil with a hexagonal barrel, curving lines incised into the clay with the end of a paper clip: there are all kinds of things to try.

I used pre-prepared enamel powders, which simply need to be mixed with water. You can use lump enamel, which has to be ground down—but ready-made powder is easier, particularly if this is your first enamel project. I chose three colours in the blue–green part of the spectrum, as these tend to be the most successful and reliable. The most difficult colours to fire are the reds and yellows. If you are not sure how the colours will turn out, make a test piece first.

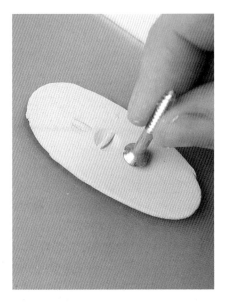

1 Roll out some clay at least four cards thick (the clay needs to be quite thick so you can make the indentations deep enough). Put a little badger balm onto the screw head, and push it carefully into the clay so it makes a clear indentation—but not so deep that it makes the clay too thin. I made four indentations, one below the other.

2 Once you are happy with the spacing, use a screwdriver bit to make one indentation at the top and one at the bottom. At the top of the earring, make a hole inside the indentation using a piece of wire. This is where the ear wire will go.

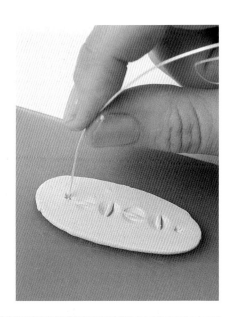

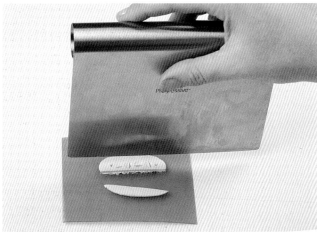

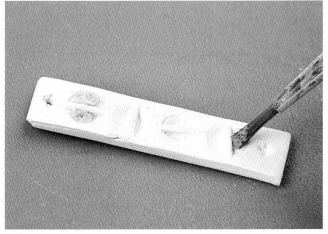

3 Using a straight metal edge, cut the clay along each side of the indentations to produce a long strip, making sure you don't cut into the indentations. Then cut off the top and bottom of the strip to form a rectangle. Repeat Steps 1 to 3 to make the other earring, matching the spacings and size as closely as possible to those of the first earring. Leave both to dry, then sand the edges and neaten the holes. Fire the earrings in the kiln on a pmc fast setting.

4 Tip a small amount of enamel powder into a dish and mix it with a little water. Dip a very fine paintbrush into the enamel and transfer it into the first indentation. When you have applied colour to all the indentations, leave the earrings to dry. Make sure that you wash the brush well between colours.

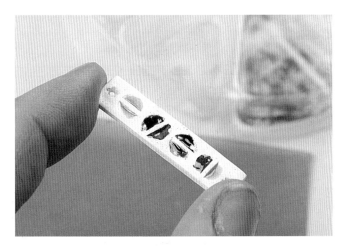

5 Fire the earrings on a pmc fast setting. If the enamel looks patchy when the earrings come out of the kiln, add more enamel on top of the fired enamel and refire the piece at the same setting; you may need to do this several times. Traditionally, you should fill the indents completely until they are flush with the silver; I left them half full, but you can continue up to the top if you wish. When you are happy with the finish, put the earrings in the barrel polisher for an hour.

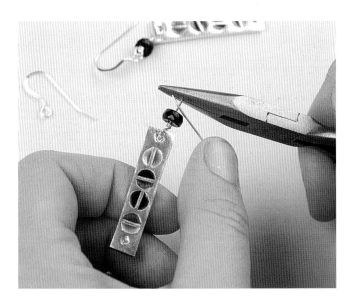

VARIATION

A star-shaped indent in these earrings provides a perfect opportunity for enamellling. You can use whatever shape you like, but make sure the clay is not too thin.

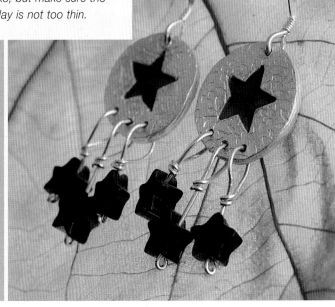

6 Cut a 1¼-in. (3-cm) length of 24-gauge (0.6mm) silver wire. Using round-nose pliers, form a closed loop at one end (see page 20). Thread on your chosen bead (I chose a bead to match one of the enamel colours), then push the unlooped end of the wire through the top hole in the earring. Form another closed loop, at right angles to the first. Hold the loop with flat-nose pliers, wrap the excess wire around the bottom of the loop to secure it, and then trim off the excess wire with wire cutters. Using flat-nose pliers, open up the loop at the bottom of the ear wire, link it onto the top loop of the earring, and close it up securely. Repeat to complete the second earring.

KEUM-BOO
LEAF EARRINGS

MATERIALS
small packet pmc3 clay
24ct keum-boo gold foil
pair of silver sleepers

TOOLS
badger balm
workboard
roller and spacers
skeleton leaf
skewer or large eyelet
butane torch and heatproof mat
  or fire brick, or kiln
pen
scissors
hot plate
burnishing tool
tweezers
wire brush
rubber block
Platinol
paintbrush
fine sandpaper
round needle file

Keum-boo is a traditional Korean technique of applying pure gold foil to fine silver. Here, I've used the gold foil to create a simple leaf shape, which forms a dramatic contrast to the silver. This is a very economical way of using gold.

The foil that is used for keum-boo is available from pmc suppliers. It is different to the foil used in calligraphy; it is a little thicker. The technique requires a little practice, but it is well worth the effort. The gold foil comes packed between two layers of card to protect it from damage; you can draw your design on this card and cut it out with a pair of sharp scissors.

1 Rub a little badger balm on your hands and tools. Measure out two equal balls of clay, using slightly less than half the packet for each earring, and roll each one into an elongated oval about 1½ in. (4 cm) tall. (It doesn't matter if they are slightly different shapes and sizes.) Place the leaf skeleton on top of one piece, gently roll over the top, and peel the leaf away to reveal the texture. Repeat for the other earring.

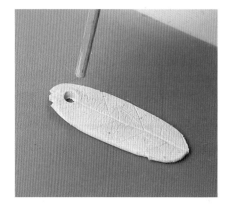

2 Using a skewer or a large eyelet, make a hole at the top of each earring. Leave the earrings to dry. Don't sand the edges; leave them rough. Fire the earrings either in a kiln on a pmc fast setting or with a butane torch on a heatproof mat or fire brick (see page 12).

3 Take the gold foil, but don't take it out of the cardboard yet. Draw two leaf shapes on the cardboard that backs the gold foil, estimating the length against the earring, and cut out the shapes with a pair of scissors.

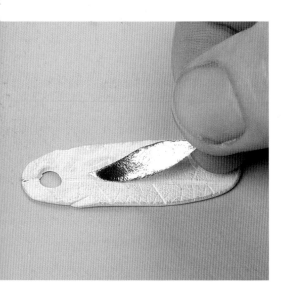

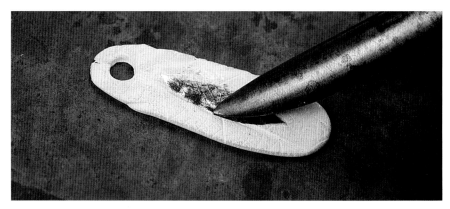

4 Using tweezers, carefully remove the gold foil from the cardboard backing. Place the shapes on the fired clay.

5 Place one earring on the hot plate and turn it to a high setting. Put on some tight-fitting gardening gloves to protect your hands, as it gets very hot working so close to the hot plate. When the hot plate reaches the required temperature, gently rub the burnishing tool over the middle of the gold shape, gradually working your way out to the edges (see page 16). (Use a pair of tweezers to hold the earring still while you work.) Repeat for the other earring.

6 When the earrings have cooled down, polish them with a wire brush. (The burnishing marks will disappear with polishing.)

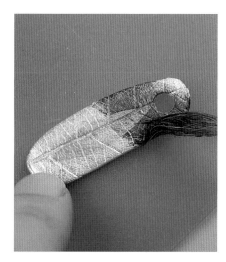

7 Mix a weak solution of Platinol (see page 18), and paint it over the surface of the leaves to bring out their texture.

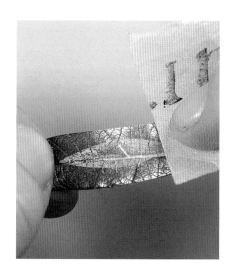

8 Gently rub over the top with a fine piece of sandpaper to highlight the surface. In this example, only half has been cleaned to leave a contrasting, grainy section.

9 Fix the sleepers through the holes in the tops of the earrings. If the holes aren't big enough, enlarge them with a round needle file.

VARIATION

This dramatic butterfly pendant has gold-foil "spots" on the wings and is hung on cord strung with tiny star-shaped pearls.

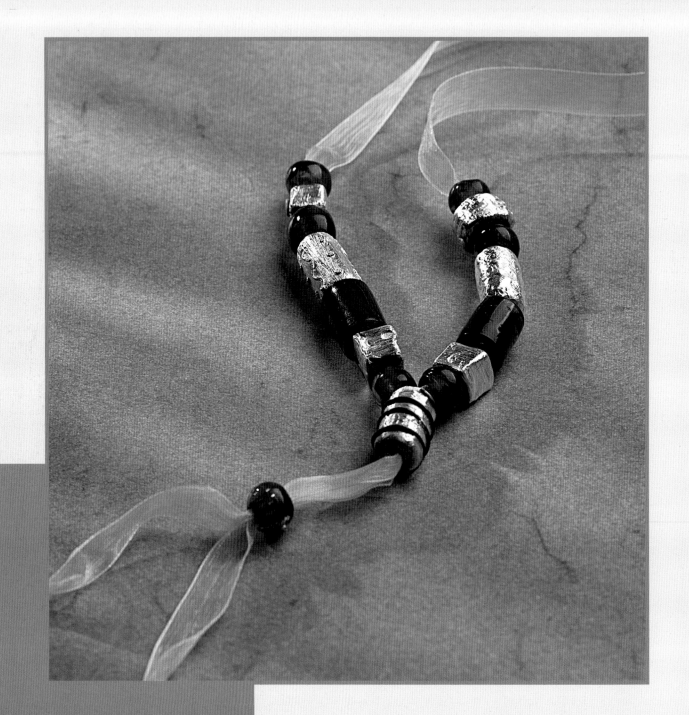

B I S Q U E
BEADS

MATERIALS
pmc3 slip
pmc3 syringe
thin copper wire
3 x 20mm cylinder bisque beads
4 x 10mm square bisque beads
7 x 8mm round glass beads
2 x l2mm cylinder beads
30-in. (75-cm) length of ¹/₂-in.
   (13-mm) ribbon with clasp attached

TOOLS
skewers
masking tape
paintbrush
wire cutters
kiln
wire brush and rubber block
scissors

This bead necklace, in which pmc is painted or syringed onto unglazed ceramic (bisque) beads to form a silver pattern, is a very economical way of using pmc to create highly individual beads. There are many different shapes and sizes of unglazed beads available, including pendant shapes. If you want your beads to have a smoother finish than mine, build up the slip in thin layers, sanding between layers, before you apply a design.

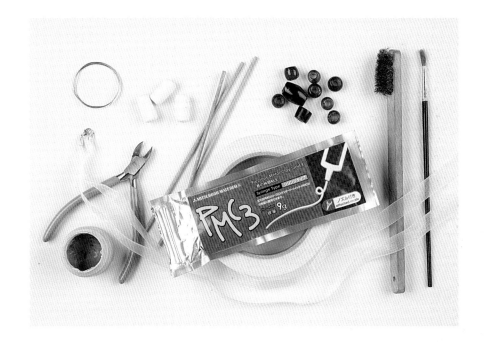

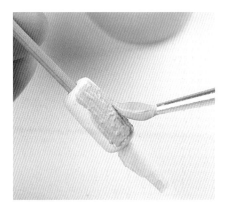

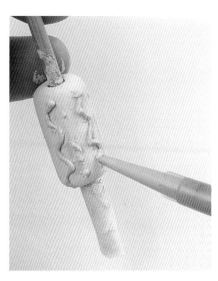

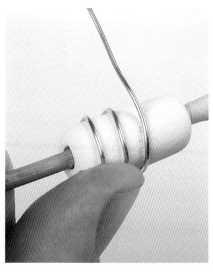

1 Place the ready-made cylinder beads on a skewer, then tape masking tape over the end of the skewer so that the beads cannot fall off. Paint the whole of the first bead in a thick, quite rough layer of slip, so that it has peaks and troughs, then leave it to dry.

2 Using syringe pmc, pipe a wiggly line down the length of the second bead, with three dots at the side. Repeat the pattern around the bead, then leave to dry.

3 For the final cylinder bead, wind a length of copper tightly around the bead, and then trim it to length.

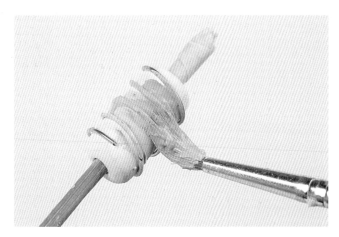

4 Paint slip over the top of the wire and all over the bead, then leave it to dry. When it is dry, sand the top edge of the wire to remove the slip and reveal the copper.

5 Paint the rest of the ceramic beads as you wish, then leave them to dry. Once they are dry, place the beads in the kiln and fire them on a pmc slow setting. Leave the beads to cool, then polish with a wire brush for a satin finish.

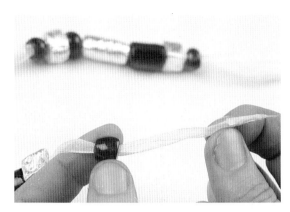

7 Thread both pieces of ribbon through the last cylinder bead, so that it hangs vertically.

6 Cut the ribbon in half. Alternating glass and silver bisque beads, and placing a long cylinder bead in the center, thread the same pattern of beads onto each length of ribbon. (Wrap a small piece of masking tape around one end of the ribbon to make it easier to thread on the beads.)

VARIATION

This bracelet uses hand-made bisque beads in irregular shapes, combined with an asymmetrical mix of carnelian, Egyptian paste, and millefiore beads.

8 Add a glass bead and tie several knots in the end of the ribbon to secure it. The ribbon I used had a ready-made clasp attached, but you could use two silver callottes and add a silver clasp, as described in the Ribboned Heart Bead on page 86.

GUSTAV KLIMT
PENDANT

MATERIALS

large packet pmc3 clay
cork clay
pmc3 slip
pmc3 syringe
1 x 5mm triangular red
  cubic zirconia
2 x 3mm round green cubic
  zirconias

keum-boo gold foil
enamel powders in three
  colours
Platinol
1x silver headpin
18 in. (45 cm) coloured cord

TOOLS

sketchbook and pen
paper
scissors
acetate for template
3-in. (7–8-cm) length of
  20-gauge (0.8mm)
  silver wire
wire cutters
round-nose pliers
flat-nose pliers
non-stick plastic
badger balm
workboard
roller and spacers
craft knife
film canister
round needle file
flat needle file
sandpaper

fine paintbrush
rubber blending tool
kiln
tweezers
hot plate
burnishing tool
barrel polisher

This project aims to give you ideas on how to start designing your own jewellery. It is very tempting to look at other people's jewellery designs for inspiration—but to start designing pieces that are truly your own, you need to look at designing in a different way. Choose something that interests you and look at every aspect of it. This design was inspired by the paintings of Gustav Klimt, an artist working in Austria at the start of the 20th century. His work lends itself well to jewellery design because he uses great patterns as backgrounds and uses a lot of colour and gold leaf. I looked at elements in Klimt's work that I thought would translate well into jewellery design. I cut a square frame out of paper to highlight areas of pattern that I liked and drew them. I concentrated on the overall texture and pattern of the detail from the painting—circles, triangles, and spirals. I decided to keep the shape simple to show off the pattern, and chose a triangle as the basic pendant shape, as triangles feature a lot in Klimt's paintings.

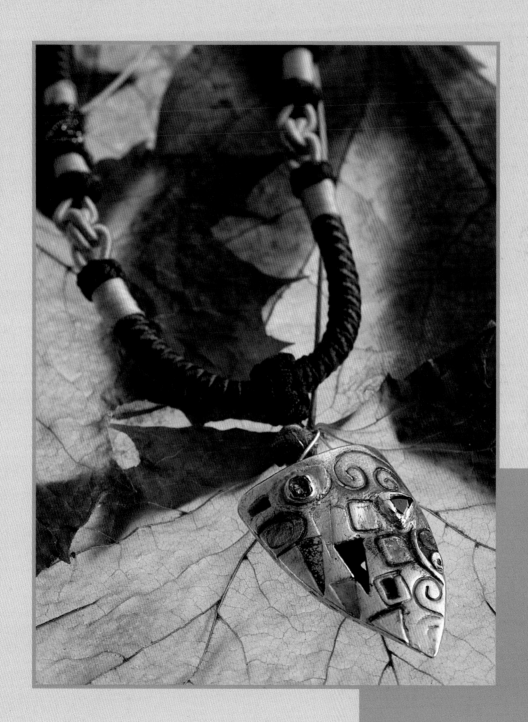

1 Begin by selecting your reference material as a starting point. Look at all the different shapes used in the detailing. One way of doing this is to cut a small paper frame and lay it over different areas of the picture; this can help you to narrow down the elements that you want to use. Note down any ideas that you have regarding colours, particular jewellery-making techniques, and so on.

2 When you've decided on a basic shape for the pendant, cut out different versions of the shape in paper. Once you have made your final choice, cut out the same shape from acetate. You also need to think about what you are going to suspend the pendant from, so that you can incorporate any fittings from the outset. I found a green, gold, and red cord that goes well with the colours of the enamel and the gold foil.

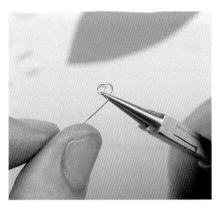

3 To impress patterns into the clay, shape wire into spirals (see page 19), and cut tiny triangles, squares, and circles from acetate. Another option is to draw a design and get it made into a rubber stamp to create the texture.

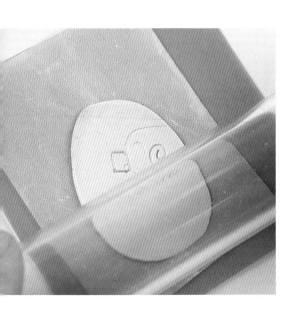

4 Place a sheet of non-stick plastic on the workboard. Rub badger balm on your hands and tools, then roll out a piece of clay to slightly larger than the acetate template, and at least three playing cards thick. Place the spirals of wire and acetate shapes on top, then gently roll over the top to impress the patterns. (It is easiest to impress one shape at a time.) Hold the acetate template over the top of the clay, to see where you need to decorate.

5 When you are pleased with the texturing, place the acetate template on top of the clay. Using a craft knife, cut around the template and remove the excess clay. (I also cut out a triangle from the center of the design.) Try not to cut the triangle too near the edge.

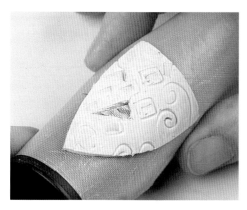

6 Pick up the non-stick plastic and clay, and place them on a curved surface so that the clay dries in that shape. I used an empty film canister; if necessary, fix the plastic in place with masking tape.

7 When the clay is dry, take it off the non-stick plastic, file the edges, and slightly bevel the edge inwards all the way around. Take some cork clay and press it onto the back of the triangle. (Try not to make the cork clay too thick, otherwise the back won't fit.) Leave the pendant in a warm place to let the cork clay dry out. It must dry for at least 24 hours. The cork clay will ensure that the piece holds its shape while it is being fired.

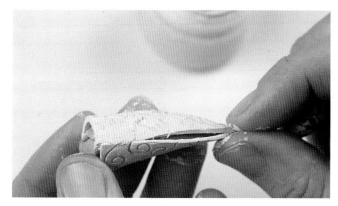

8 Repeat the process to make a second triangle for the back of the pendant. To join them together, paint slip on the join and on the cork clay. Lay the back piece on the cork clay, line up the edges, and smooth them together. Add extra slip if necessary to ensure that the pieces are well joined, so that the piece does not split during firing. Leave the pendant to dry, then file and sand the edges. If you remove any of the pattern while filing, scratch it back in afterwards. File the top edge straight or with a slight inward curve.

9 Roll out some more clay and impress the wire spirals into it to make a pattern. Carefully turn the clay over so that it is pattern side down, then gently place the pendant on top. Using a craft knife, cut around the pendant to create a leaf shape (this will be the top of the pendant). Paint slip along the open edge of the triangular piece, then place the leaf-shaped piece pattern side up on top. Using the rubber blending tool, smooth over the join. Leave to dry, then fill any visible join with slip. Leave to dry again, then file and sand the join.

10 Using a piece of wire, make a hole in the leaf-shaped top of the pendant.

11 Cut a couple of small triangles of pmc and apply them with slip to the front and back of the pendant. Using the end of a round file or drill bit, make a small hole where the stones are to go. Put a dab of slip under each stone and put the stone in the hole. Roll a small sausage of clay and wrap it around the edge of the stone, making sure you have covered the widest part. Neaten the piece as much as you can and leave it to dry. When it is dry, sand around the edges and make sure there is no clay on the top of the stones. Fire the piece in a kiln on a pmc3 fast setting.

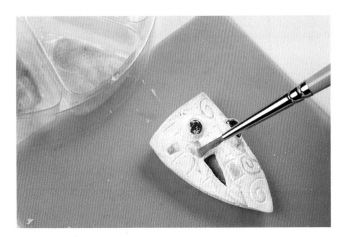

12 Mix the enamel powders with water. Using a fine paintbrush, apply the colours to selected indentations on the pendant. Leave the piece to dry. Fire in a kiln on a pmc3 fast setting. You may need to add another layer of enamel and fire again (see page 15).

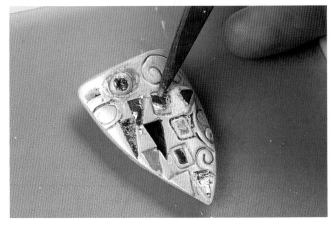

13 Cut out the shapes you want from the gold foil. Using tweezers, remove the foil from its cardboard backing and place it on the pendant. Place the pendant on the hot plate, turn it on to the high setting, and wait for it to heat up. Put on some tight-fitting gardening gloves. When the hot plate reaches the correct temperature, use a burnishing tool to rub the gold foil onto the surface (see page 16). (Use a pair of tweezers to hold the pendant still while you work).

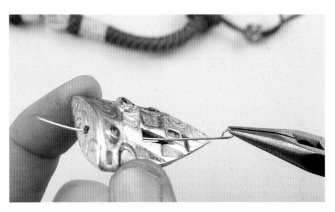

14 Polish the pendant in the barrel polisher for about an hour; if the steel shot in the barrel polisher gets stuck inside the pendant, just shake it out of the triangular hole. Mix up a weak solution of Platinol and water and paint it onto areas of the pendant that you want to darken (see page 18). Afterwards, you can put it back into the barrel polisher to polish the raised areas that have been darkened by the Platinol and highlight the silver. Use very fine sandpaper to polish highlights in certain places—around the stones, for example.

15 Now you can attach the pendant to the cord. Feed the silver headpin through the triangular hole and out through the hole at the top. If the hole is too big for the head pin, put a bead on the end before you thread it in.

16 Using round-nose pliers, curl the other end of the headpin over the cord in a loop. Then wrap the wire around the bottom of the loop to create a closed loop (see page 20), and trim off any excess wire.

INDEX

This index gives page references to the projects and techniques found in the book. Page numbers in *italics* refer to illustrations. As many of the same techniques are used throughout the book, the page references are intended to direct the reader to substantial entries only.

CREDITS

The author would like to thank The PMC Studio for supplying materials. They can be contacted at www.thepmcstudio.com.

Breslich & Foss Ltd would like to thank the following individuals for their help in the creation of this book:

Commissioning Editor: Janet Ravenscroft
Copy Editing: Sarah Hoggett
Design: Janet James
Editorial assistance: Jane Birch
Illustrations: Kuo Kang Chen
Photography: Martin Norris